STECK-VAUGHN

PreGED
Critical Thinking Skills

REVIEWERS

Robert Christensen
Principal
Handlon Correctional Facility
Michigan Department
of Corrections
Ionia, MI

Arnoldo Hinojosa
Senior Director
Community Initiatives
Harris County Department
of Education
Houston, TX

Linda Correnti
GED Staff Developer
Alternative Schools & Programs
New York City Department
of Education
New York, NY

Nancy Lawrence
E-teacher
KC Distance Learning, Inc.
Butler, PA

Dr. Gary A. Eyre
Consultant
GED Testing Service
Advance Associates
and Consultants
Phoenix, AZ

Charan Lee
Director
Adult Education
Anderson School Districts 1 & 2
Williamston, SC

Harcourt Achieve

Rigby · Saxon · Steck-Vaughn

www.HarcourtAchieve.com
1.800.531.5015

Executive Editor: Ellen Northcutt

Senior Editor: Donna Townsend

Associate Design Director: Joyce Spicer

Senior Designer: Jim Cauthron

Senior Photo Researcher: Alyx Kellington

Editorial Development: Learning Unlimited, Oak Park, IL

Photography Credits: p. 7 © Sakurai/Cartoonists and Writers Syndicate; p. 12 © Laima Druskis/Stock Boston; p. 54 © Michael Keller/CORBIS; p. 60, 61a Courtesy of U.S. National Archives and Records Administration; p. 61b Courtesy of Library of Congress; p. 62 Photo Communications, Inc., Courtesy of U.S. National Archives and Records Administration; p. 63 Courtesy of Franklin D. Roosevelt Presidential Library; p. 88 © Jim Morin/King Features Syndicate; p. 89a © John Sherffius/St. Louis Post-Dispatch; p. 89b © Wayne Stayskal/The Tampa Tribune; p. 90 © Rex Babin/The Sacramento Bee; p. 91 © Steve Breen/The Ashbury Park Press/Copley News Service; p. 93 © Daryl Cagle of Slate/MSN; p. 95 Courtesy of the U.S. National Archives and Records Administration; p. 96 © Mary Kate Denny/PhotoEdit Inc.; p. 140 Courtesy of the National Oceanic and Atmospheric Administration; p. 142 © Milt Priggee/www.miltpriggee.com.

Acknowledgments for literary selections are on page 174, which is an extension of this copyright page.

ISBN 0-7398-6701-6

10 11 12   1689   14 13 12 11
4500297527

CONTENTS

How to Use This Book

The purpose of this book is to help you practice the critical thinking and graphic skills you will need to answer questions on the GED Language Arts, Reading; Social Studies; and Science Tests. On these tests, you will have to use the following thinking skills to answer questions about passages or graphics.

- Comprehension – understanding information in a passage or graphic
- Application – using what you understand in a specific or new context
- Analysis – interpreting different aspects of what you read or see in a graphic
- Synthesis – putting together different information to form a new idea
- Evaluation – determining support for a conclusion or identifying bias or other viewpoints

You will also need to be able to interpret the following kinds of graphics.

- Tables
- Charts
- Graphs
- Diagrams
- Maps
- Political Cartoons
- Photographs

You will want to know how to use the following features to make the most of this book.

Pretest and Pretest Evaluation Chart

Take the Prestest to see how you do with the types of skills you will need to pass the GED. You will be well-prepared if you work through this entire book. However, you may also use the Pretest Evaluation Chart to identify only the pages related to the skills that were problems for you on the Pretest.

Units and Lessons

This book consists of three units—Reading, Social Studies, and Science— that are divided into lessons. Each lesson focuses on a specific thinking or graphic skill for that content area.

The left-hand page of each lesson teaches you the skill, gives you some sample questions with feedback, shows you a graphic organizer to use with the skill, and provides you with useful tips for using the skill.

The right-hand page allows you to practice the skill, use the graphic organizer, and apply it to GED-type questions. Since half or more of the questions on the GED Social Studies and Science Tests are based on graphics, the two units for these content areas contain special **Graphic Skills** lessons that help you to interpret information from visual sources, such as graphs and maps.

Skill Practices

At the end of a group of lessons, you will practice the skills that you learned. This type of cumulative review will help you remember the skills you have learned in the preceding lessons. It will also give you a chance to practice with questions that are like the ones on the GED Test.

Mini-Tests

These tests at the end of each unit allow you to practice GED-type questions in each content area in a timed testing situation.

Posttest and Posttest Evaluation Chart

A Posttest allows you to apply the skills you have learned in all three units to GED-type questions. You can compare your results on the Posttest with your Pretest results to see how much progress you have made.

Answers and Explanations

Use this section at the back of the book to check your work and to learn why the correct answers are correct. You will also find here a completed sample of the graphic organizer for each lesson. Compare the sample to your own to see if yours is similar.

This Pretest will help you to determine the GED critical thinking skills that you need to develop. Complete the Pretest and check your answers on pages 149–150. Then use the Pretest Evaluation Chart on page 11 to plan your work in this book.

Unit 1: Reading

Directions: Choose the one best answer to each question.

Questions 1 through 3 refer to the following excerpt from a novel.

HOW DOES THE FAMILY REACT?

Before Ben could answer, Bull thundered out at all of them, "I'm gonna give you hogs about five seconds to cut the yappin' then I'm gonna pull this car over to the side of the
(5) road and I bet I can shut your yaps even if your mother can't."

"Hush," Lillian hissed at her children. "Not another sound." Her eyes cast a stern, desperate communiqué to her children.
(10) But this time there was no need. Bull's tone had registered. Each child knew the exact danger signals in the meteorology [science of weather] of their father's temperament; they were adroit weathermen
(15) who charted the clouds, winds, and high pressure areas of his fiercely wavering moods, with skill created through long experience. His temper was quick fused and uncontrollable and once he passed a certain
(20) point, not even Lillian could calm him. He was tired now after driving through half the night. Behind his sunglasses, the veined eyes were thinned with fatigue and a most dangerous ice had formed over them. The
(25) threshing winds of his temper buffeted the car and deep, resonant warning signals were sent out among the children. Silence ruled them in an instant. They resumed watching the diminishing countryside on the outskirts
(30) of Ravenel. "Control," Lillian said soothingly.

"Control is very important for all of us." She was looking at her husband.

Pat Conroy, *The Great Santini*

1. Which of the following best expresses the main idea of the passage?
   (1) People's moods are like the weather.
   (2) Children should always have respect for their fathers.
   (3) The father shouldn't be driving half of the night.
   (4) The mother understands that control is very important.
   (5) The children and wife are fearful of the father's temper.

2. What can be inferred about Lillian's feelings toward the children?
   (1) She wants to protect them from their father.
   (2) She feels she can't control them.
   (3) She doesn't care if the father yells at them.
   (4) She's afraid the children will continue to be noisy.
   (5) She wishes she weren't so calm.

3. How would Bull most likely respond if he were served the wrong meal at a restaurant?
   (1) kindly ask for the correct meal
   (2) take the meal without saying a word
   (3) let his wife handle the situation
   (4) yell at his kids that it was their fault
   (5) get upset with the waiter

Questions 4 through 6 refer to the following section from an employee handbook.

WHAT ARE THE BENEFITS OF JOB SHARING AND PART-TIME EMPLOYMENT?

Fulton Lumber Personnel Policies

This section provides information for employees who are considering part-time employment or job sharing. We believe that offering employees a variety of personnel

(5) options helps to achieve a family-friendly workplace. Employees should consider the following information when thinking about reducing their work hours.

Part-time employment

(10) A part-time, permanent employee works between 16 and 32 hours each week on a prearranged schedule. Part-time permanent employees are eligible for health and insurance benefits, as well as family leave

(15) and retirement once they have built up enough hours.

Job sharing

Job sharing is a form of part-time employment. Most job-sharing teams are at

(20) the same job classification. The schedules of two or more part-time employees are arranged to cover the duties of one full-time position (40 hours a week). However, job sharing does not necessarily mean that each

(25) job-sharer must work half-time, or 20 hours a week.

Who benefits?

Both employees and managers benefit from part-time work schedules. Employees can

(30) spend more time with their children, pursue educational opportunities, care for an aging or ill family member, or continue working when illness or physical limitations prevent

working full-time. Managers can retain

(35) highly-qualified employees, improve recruitment, increase productivity, and reduce absenteeism.

4. What would happen if an employee who is job sharing could only work 18 hours?
    (1) The employee would not receive benefits.
    (2) The employee would be fired.
    (3) The employee would be demoted.
    (4) The other job-sharer would work 22 hours.
    (5) The job-sharer would take family leave.

5. Which statement supports Fulton Lumber's opinion that job sharing and part-time work mean a family-friendly workplace?
    (1) Most jobs that are shared are at the same job classification.
    (2) Job-sharers and part-time employees have benefits and flexible hours.
    (3) Job sharing and part-time employment improves recruitment and productivity.
    (4) Employees have to work 20 hours.
    (5) Job-sharers and part-time employees have prearranged schedules.

6. Which of the following best describes the tone of the handbook?
    (1) humorous
    (2) intimidating
    (3) sarcastic
    (4) business-like
    (5) disrespectful

   Go on to the next page.

Unit 2: Social Studies

Questions 7 and 8 refer to the following map of Michigan.

7. According to the map, which geographical feature makes Michigan unique?

    (1) its extensive system of rivers
    (2) its huge size, compared to that of neighboring states
    (3) its many Great Lakes shorelines
    (4) its absence of natural harbors
    (5) its narrow coastal mountain range

8. If you were traveling from Green Bay to Detroit by the most direct route possible, in what order would you pass through Ann Arbor, Chicago, Kalamazoo and Milwaukee?

    (1) Ann Arbor, Chicago, Kalamazoo, and Milwaukee
    (2) Milwaukee, Chicago, Kalamazoo, and Ann Arbor
    (3) Milwaukee, Chicago, Ann Arbor, and Kalamazoo
    (4) Ann Arbor, Milwaukee, Chicago, Kalamazoo
    (5) Ann Arbor, Kalamazoo, Chicago, and Milwaukee

Questions 9 and 10 refer to the following information.

The first woman elected to Congress was Jeannette Rankin. Born in Montana in 1880, Rankin helped win Montana women the vote six years before the Nineteenth Amendment gave women that right nationwide. In 1916 Rankin was elected to Congress. She soon faced a vote on a declaration of war on Germany. She responded, "I want to stand for my country, but I cannot vote for war." A generation later, Rankin was the only representative to vote against the declaration of war on Japan. She remained a pacifist until her death in 1973, and even marched to protest the Vietnam War.

9. Which statement best summarizes this passage?

    (1) Rankin helped women in Montana win the vote.
    (2) Jeannette Rankin took a strong stand on the causes that mattered to her.
    (3) Jeannette Rankin served in Congress.
    (4) Jeannette Rankin devoted her later life to a variety of humanitarian causes.
    (5) Congress has the power to declare war.

10. Why did Rankin vote against the entry of the United States into both world wars?

    (1) She opposed war in general.
    (2) She opposed the President's views.
    (3) She feared, in both cases, that the United States would lose.
    (4) She was trying to get publicity.
    (5) She wanted the money that would be spent on war to be used elsewhere.

Questions 11 and 12 refer to the following political cartoon.

SAKURAI
RECKLINGHAUSER ZEITUNG
Recklinghausen
GERMANY

CARTOONISTS & WRITERS SYNDICATE http://CartoonWeb.com

11. What is the purpose of this cartoon?

   To show that

   (1) the world's people cannot be divided into the "haves" and the "have nots"
   (2) farmers produce enough food to support the world's population
   (3) the rich have a duty to improve the living conditions of the poor
   (4) countries that are well-off are ignoring problems of poverty and starvation in other parts of the world
   (5) cleaning up the environment is everyone's responsibility

12. Which international organization would be most likely to address the problem that this cartoon illustrates?

   (1) the World Meteorological Organization
   (2) the World Bank
   (3) the International Olympic Committee
   (4) the World Wildlife Fund
   (5) Action Against Hunger

Questions 13 and 14 refer to the following information.

Aside from serving as fuel, what good is oil? Countries that produce oil have discovered that this natural resource has many benefits.

Leaders of some oil-rich countries have used money from the sale of oil to improve the lives of their people. For example, oil money can be used to build schools and hire teachers, import food, and raise the quality of medical care. Some leaders have used their control of oil exports to gain political or economic power in the world. Occasionally oil-producing countries have cut the amount of oil exported—that is, have imposed an embargo—as a way of protesting another country's actions or a political situation that they did not like.

13. Based on the information in the passage, which statement is an opinion?
    (1) Some countries use oil to "buy" themselves a political voice.
    (2) Oil money has been used to improve people's lives.
    (3) Building schools is a wise use of oil money.
    (4) Embargoes have been used as a form of political protest.
    (5) Oil is an important natural resource.

14. If an oil embargo were imposed against the United States, what change do you predict would take place at your local gas station?
    (1) Another form of fuel would go on sale.
    (2) The federal government would take over the running of the gas station.
    (3) The gas station would have to close.
    (4) The price of gasoline would fall.
    (5) The price of gasoline would rise.

Unit 3: Science

Question 15 refers to the following information.

A farmer noticed that one pond on his farm had no algae growing in it. The other pond had a thick growth of algae. He hypothesized that the pond without algae contained very little nitrogen, a nutrient needed by algae. He collected a sample of water from each pond and had the samples analyzed for their nitrogen content. The analysis showed that the sample from the pond with algae contained much more nitrogen than the sample from the pond without algae. This result supported the farmer's hypothesis.

15. What observation led to the farmer's hypothesis?

   (1) There were two ponds on the farm.
   (2) One pond contained very little nitrogen.
   (3) One pond had no algae growing in it.
   (4) Both ponds contained water.
   (5) Nitrogen is a nutrient needed by algae.

Question 16 refers to the following information.

Tiny organisms called yeasts and bacteria are used to make many foods. For example, leavened bread is made by adding yeast to dough. The yeast produces carbon dioxide gas, which makes the dough rise. Cheese is made by adding certain bacteria to milk. The bacteria produce lactic acid, which sours the milk.

16. What is the effect of adding yeast to dough?

   (1) The dough rises.
   (2) The dough produces carbon dioxide gas.
   (3) The dough turns into cheese.
   (4) The yeast turns into bacteria.
   (5) The yeast produces lactic acid.

Questions 17 and 18 refer to the following information and diagram.

When you look through the viewfinder of an SLR camera, you see the light that enters the camera through the lens. A mirror in the camera deflects the incoming light toward the viewfinder. When you press the shutter button, the mirror moves out of the way, and the light strikes the film.

Path of Light Through an SLR Camera

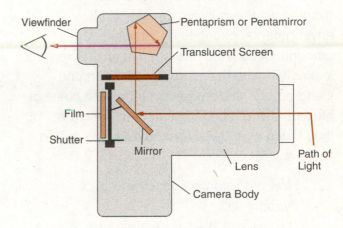

17. What is the topic of the diagram?

   (1) how film moves through an SLR camera
   (2) how light passes through an SLR camera
   (3) how to build an SLR camera
   (4) how to repair an SLR camera
   (5) how to take photographs with a camera

18. According to the diagram, what happens to the light after it hits the mirror?

   (1) It is absorbed by the mirror.
   (2) It bounces off the shutter.
   (3) It strikes the film.
   (4) It enters the lens.
   (5) It passes through a translucent screen.

Questions 19 and 20 refer to the following information.

Dinosaurs appeared on Earth about 230 million years ago. They became extinct about 65 million years ago. Several ideas have been proposed to explain why dinosaurs became extinct. One is that the environment changed gradually and dinosaurs could not adapt to the change. Another idea, called the "impact hypothesis," says that an asteroid or comet collided with Earth. According to this hypothesis, the collision caused rapid environmental changes by throwing large amounts of dust into the atmosphere. Scientists looked for evidence of such a collision and found a huge underwater crater off the coast of Mexico. Using techniques to date the crater, they found that it was formed about 65 million years ago.

19. How did scientists test the impact hypothesis?

    (1) They examined dinosaurs that lived in Mexico.
    (2) They created a crater in Mexico.
    (3) They looked for evidence of a huge asteroid or comet collision.
    (4) They created a large asteroid or comet collision on computers.
    (5) They began studying the fossils of dinosaurs.

20. What information presented in the passage supports the impact hypothesis?

    (1) A large crater was formed about 65 million years ago.
    (2) No comets have collided with Earth for 65 million years.
    (3) Dinosaurs appeared about 230 million years ago.
    (4) Comets are made of ice and dust.
    (5) No other animals have become extinct.

Questions 21 and 22 refer to the following information and graph.

When two minerals are rubbed together, the harder mineral will scratch the softer one. The harder a mineral is, the more durable it is. The hardness of minerals is measured by the Mohs scale.

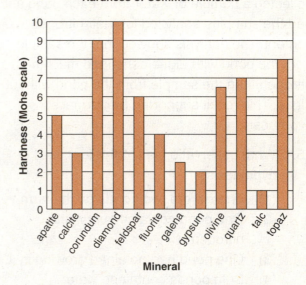

Hardness of Common Minerals

21. Which of the following restates a fact shown in the graph?

    (1) Calcite is harder than olivine.
    (2) Fluorite is harder than corundum.
    (3) Topaz is harder than diamond.
    (4) Gypsum is softer than feldspar.
    (5) Apatite is softer than galena.

22. Which mineral would make the longest-lasting grinding surface?

    (1) apatite
    (2) diamond
    (3) quartz
    (4) talc
    (5) topaz

Pretest Evaluation Chart

After you have completed the Pretest, check your answers on pages 149–150. On the chart below, circle the number of each question that you answered correctly on the Pretest. Count the number of questions you answered correctly in each row. Write the number in the Total Correct space in each row. (For example, in the Reading: Comprehension row, write the number correct in the blank before *out of 2*) Complete this process for the remaining rows.

Content Area	Questions	Total Correct	Pages
Unit 1: Reading			
Comprehension	1, 2	_____ out of 2	14–19
Application	3	_____ out of 1	44–45
Analysis	4, 5	_____ out of 2	22–27, 30–31, 36–39
Synthesis	6	_____ out of 1	32–33, 40–41, 46–47
	TOTAL	_____ **out of 6**	
Unit 2: Social Studies			
Comprehension	**7**, 9	_____ out of 2	56–59
Application	**12**	_____ out of 1	78–79
Analysis	**8**, 13, 14	_____ out of 3	64–69, 76–77
Evaluation	10, **11**	_____ out of 2	74–75, 84–87
	TOTAL	_____ **out of 8**	
Unit 3: Science			
Comprehension	**17**, 21	_____ out of 2	98–101
Application	**22**	_____ out of 1	118–119
Analysis	16, **18**, 19	_____ out of 3	106–111, 116–117
Evaluation	15, 20	_____ out of 2	124–127
	TOTAL	_____ **out of 8**	

Now work through this book, focusing on the areas in which you had the most problems. When you are finished with this book, you will take a posttest to evaluate your progress with these important PreGED skills.

Question numbers that are in **bold** are based on graphics, which can be reviewed in the special graphic skills lessons.

Plan Your Work

In which areas do you need to do the most work? Page numbers to refer to for practice are given in the chart.

Reading

You already use basic thinking skills to understand whatever you read. However, you probably use other thinking skills as well. Have you ever read something and then applied the information to your own life, drawn a conclusion, made a comparison, or made a choice based on a fact or opinion? When you did so, you used more advanced thinking skills that are often called *critical* or *higher order* thinking skills.

Write the topic of something that you read to make something or to solve a problem.

_____

Write about a time when you had to compare information from different sources to make a decision.

_____

Thinking About Reading

You may not realize how often you use thinking skills in reading in your everyday life. Think about your recent activities.

Check the box for each activity you did.

☐ Did you analyze a bill to see if you were charged correctly?

☐ Did you compare items in ads or catalogues to find the best deals?

☐ Did you scan a newspaper article to get the main idea?

☐ Did you use something you learned in a new situation?

☐ Did you read a book to find out what happened to a character?

☐ Did you gather information from different sources to plan a trip?

☐ Did you follow a sequence of written directions?

Write some other activities where you have used thinking skills with materials you have read.

_____

_____

_____

Previewing the Unit

In this unit, you will learn:

● how to find the main idea and supporting details

● how to infer and compare and contrast information

● how to find cause-and-effect relationships

● how to draw conclusions and apply information

● how to determine an author's purpose and point of view

● how to synthesize information from several sources

Lesson 1	Main Idea	Lesson 8	Author's Purpose
Lesson 2	Details	Lesson 9	Setting
Lesson 3	Inference	Lesson 10	Character
Lesson 4	Sequence of Events	Lesson 11	Point of View
Lesson 5	Compare/Contrast	Lesson 12	Application
Lesson 6	Cause/Effect	Lesson 13	Synthesis
Lesson 7	Conclusions		

Main Idea

On the GED Reading Test, you will see questions about the main idea of a paragraph or reading passage. The **main idea** is the most important idea in the reading. It states the overall topic of the reading. Often, the main idea will be stated in one sentence within the passage. Look for the main idea of the passage below.

Lara finished patching the crack running through her neighbor's kitchen wall. The earthquake had awoken a leader in the usually shy Lara. Minutes after the quake, she checked her home for gas leaks and then began to assist her neighbors. She convinced her neighbors to combine and share their food and water. She even set up an old crystal radio set to hear reports from city officials.

1. Which sentence gives the most important information about Lara?

_____

2. State the main idea of the paragraph in your own words?

_____

1. The earthquake had awoken a leader awake in the usually shy Lara.
2. Your answer should contain the idea that Lara became a leader the day of the earthquake.

To find the main idea, organize the main idea and supporting details in a chart. The main idea is the central idea. The details point to the main idea.

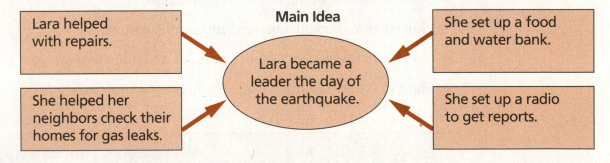

Main Idea

Lara helped with repairs.

She helped her neighbors check their homes for gas leaks.

Lara became a leader the day of the earthquake.

She set up a food and water bank.

She set up a radio to get reports.

To find the main idea in a passage, ask yourself:
- What is the most important information in the passage?
- What one sentence is most helpful in understanding the passage?

TIP

To find the main idea of a passage, imagine a friend asked you, "What are you reading about?" How would you answer your friend in one sentence? Your answer would be the main idea.

Think of a time when you listened to a friend talk about an experience. What was the most important idea about that experience?

Read the passage and complete the chart with one detail and the main idea. Then answer the questions.

Preserving photos of the past is a challenge for museum curators. They must control the humidity, light, and temperature to preserve these fragile works of art. To protect museums' collections, curators must also have some idea of how the photos were made. Most museums do not have enough money to test each photograph. Instead, curators must make reasonable guesses and hope their efforts will not destroy the artwork they seek to preserve.

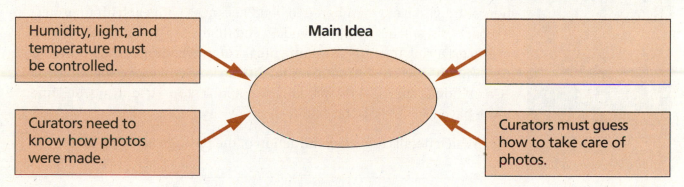

Humidity, light, and temperature must be controlled.

Main Idea

Curators need to know how photos were made.

Curators must guess how to take care of photos.

1. Imagine you are talking to a friend. In one sentence, how would you explain what this paragraph is about?

   _____

   _____

2. Which of these ideas supports the main idea of the passage?
   a. Curators must find the best way to display photos for the public.
   b. Some photos must be protected from exposure to normal air.

GED PRACTICE   Choose the **one best answer** to the question.

By the end of the season, I knew a lot about Max. He was the best shortstop I ever saw. He always convinced some friend, usually me, into hitting him ground balls late into the night. He once spent five hours in the batting cage working on his swing. Max was only 16 years old, and he was surely headed for the big leagues.

We were all surprised by the car accident in his senior year. Max shattered his right arm, his throwing arm. Some people said his career was over, but I knew he'd be back. Max was never a quitter.

3. Which of the following is the main idea of the first paragraph?

   (1) Max convinced his friends to work with him.
   (2) Max worked very hard to be a good baseball player.
   (3) Max spent five hours practicing his swing.
   (4) Max was only 16 years old.
   (5) Max was headed for the big leagues.

MAIN IDEA   Check your answers on page 150.   **15**

Details

Some questions on the GED Reading Test are based on understanding the **details** in a paragraph or passage. As you saw in Lesson 1, the details in a paragraph support the main idea. They give facts about people, places, things, times, and events. Details give life to a passage and make it more interesting for the reader. Read the passage, and look for interesting details.

Marcus felt exhausted and numb after working the second shift. He had been loading identical cardboard boxes into delivery trucks for twelve hours straight. He remembered to bend his knees with each lift to protect his back, but still his strong shoulders and thighs burned and ached with overuse. During the fifteen-minute breaks at the loading dock, his muscles became stiff and cold. Around midnight, he dozed off while standing up. "Go on home," his boss offered, but he couldn't stop. He only needed one more paycheck to move his family to a new city.

1. Which details tell *when* the action of the passage is taking place?

_____

2. Which sentence explains *why* Marcus is willing to work so hard?

_____

1. The details *twelve hours straight* and *around midnight* tell us that Marcus has worked all day and it is now after midnight. 2. The last sentence explains that Marcus needs money to move his family to a new city.

Details answer the questions *who, what, when, where, why,* and *how.* Use a chart to organize the details.

Who? Marcus is a strong, hard-working father.	Supporting Details	What? He is working an extra shift loading boxes.
When? He has been working all day until after midnight.	Where? He is working at a loading dock.	Why or How? Marcus wants to move his family to a new city.

To find the details in a passage, ask yourself:
- What information helps me understand the main idea?
- What information makes the passage more interesting?

Think of a television show you like to watch. What details about the characters make the show interesting?

Read the passage and complete the chart by filling in the three missing details. Then answer the questions.

Sunrise found Detective Leo Stuart ready with a shovel and pickaxe. He began digging ten feet due east of the ancient bronze marker. It did not take long before Stuart's shovel struck something hollow. Within fifteen minutes, he had removed the antique hardwood chest from its hiding place in the hillside. The chest was bound by strong iron bands. After much effort, he broke the final band. The chest sprang open to reveal nothing but a dollar bill. Scrawled across the face of the bill was the message, "Too late!" Stuart threw his shovel in frustration.

Who? Leo Stuart is a detective.	Supporting Details	What?
When?	Where?	Why or How? He is searching for something.

1. What details describe the exact place where Inspector Stuart began digging?

   _____

2. Before the chest is open, what detail suggests that the chest will be empty?

   _____

GED PRACTICE Choose the **one best answer** to the question.

One of man's greatest engineering feats was inspired by a mollusk. In 1825, an engineer named Marc Brunel watched shipworms bore holes in the wood hulls of ships. These soft-bodied animals used their shells like a hard shield to push their way farther into the wood. Brunel proposed boring a tunnel under the Thames River in London by building a great shield. As workers dug, they would push the shield into the opening like the shipworms. After many delays, Brunel's plan finally worked. Today, engineers use variations of tunneling shields to build subways all over the world.

3. A shipworm is a kind of mollusk. According to the details in the passage, which of the following is the best description of a mollusk?

   (1) an animal that eats wood
   (2) a destructive animal that digs holes
   (3) a shelled animal that lives near rivers
   (4) a soft-bodied animal that lives in a shell
   (5) an animal that engineers use to dig holes

Inference

Some questions on the GED Reading Test will ask you to **infer** ideas that are not actually stated in a passage. When you infer, you apply knowledge you already have to the situation in the passage to figure out the meaning.

I won my first contest when I was 21. I worked for a month to strengthen my arm so that I could hurl that folded piece of paper as high as possible. My first throw was a disaster, but my second throw had good upward speed. At the top of the arc, the wings opened beautifully and my little sparrow began to glide, slowly spiraling to the ground. To win, I needed to beat fifteen seconds, an impossible length of time, but I did it.

1. What details help you infer that the thrown object was a paper airplane?

_____

2. Do you think the author expected to win the contest?

_____

1. A folded paper object with wings that glides through the air is a paper airplane. 2. No, the writer did not expect to win. In the last sentence, the writer describes fifteen seconds as an impossible length of time.

In the following chart, statements from the passage are followed by inferences. You can organize your thinking in the same way.

Statement ➡	Inference
• Won first contest at 21	• He has won more contests since then.
• Worked for a month	• This event required strength.
• First throw was a disaster, but second had good upward speed	• The first throw lacked speed.
• Wings opened and it began to glide	• The airplane worked.
• Needed to beat fifteen seconds	• The goal was to keep the airplane in the air as long as possible.

To make inferences, ask yourself:

● What is the author suggesting without directly stating it?

● What clues tell me how the author feels about the topic?

When a friend tells you something that happened, how do you use your own experiences to understand it?

TIP

Some GED Test questions ask which answer choice can be inferred from the passage. First, rule out any choices that cannot be supported by at least one detail from the passage.

Read the passage and complete the chart, writing two new inferences. Then answer the questions.

The Owens family thinks that their dog Riley is a problem because he begs for food. They begin every meal by giving Riley a scrap of food from their plates. They expect the dog to let them eat in peace, but he keeps begging for more. He will only stop if they shout, "Lie down!" Then Riley will lie down on the floor immediately. Naturally, the Owens give him more food from their plates as a reward. Not surprisingly, he pops up and starts begging again. Riley's owners have tried reasoning with him, but nothing works. Clearly, Riley has no desire to obey.

Statement ⟶	Inference
• His owners begin every meal by giving him a scrap of food from their plates.	• His owners have trained him to beg by feeding him at the table.
• He will only stop if they shout, "Lie down!" Then Riley lies down on the floor immediately.	•
• His owners have tried reasoning with him, but nothing works.	•

1. The owners believe that Riley is a problem dog. What details help you infer that the author does not agree with the owners?

   _____

2. Which of the following can you infer from the passage?
   a. Riley's owners don't understand how dogs learn.
   b. Riley has no desire to obey.

Choose the one best answer to the question.

200,000 healthcare workers provide "in-home supportive services" to low-income elderly and disabled persons throughout California. A recent study recommends protecting in-home healthcare workers through improved training and equipment. The study also suggests that the workers themselves need better access to healthcare services when they become injured on the job. One innovative proposal suggests that there should be written contracts between in-home healthcare workers and their clients.

3. An organization conducted this study and made the recommendations. You can infer that this organization works on behalf of which people?

   (1) senior citizens
   (2) low-income families
   (3) in-home healthcare workers
   (4) disabled workers
   (5) California elected officials

Reading Practice 1

Directions: Choose the <u>one best answer</u> to each question.

<u>Questions 1 through 3</u> refer to the following excerpt from a novel.

WHICH INSTRUMENT IS EASIER TO LEARN?

A harmonica is easy to carry. Take it out of your hip pocket, knock it against your palm to shake out the dirt and pocket fuzz and bits of tobacco. Now
(5) it's ready. You can do anything with a harmonica: thin reedy single tone, or chords, or melody with rhythm chords. You can mold the music with curved hands, making it wail and cry like
(10) bagpipes, making it full and round like an organ, making it as sharp and bitter as the reed pipes of the hills. And you can play and put it back in your pocket. It is always with you, always in your
(15) pocket. And as you play, you learn new tricks, new ways to mold the tone with your hands, to pinch the tone with your lips, and no one teaches you. You feel around—sometimes alone in the shade
(20) at noon, sometimes in the tent door after supper when the women are washing up. Your foot taps gently on the ground. Your eyebrows rise and fall in rhythm. And if you lose it or break it,
(25) why, it's no great loss. You can buy another for a quarter.

A guitar is more precious. Must learn this thing. Fingers of the left hand must have callus caps. Thumb of the right
(30) hand a horn of callus. Stretch the left-hand fingers, stretch them like a spider's legs to get the hard pads on the frets.

John Steinbeck, *The Grapes of Wrath*

1. Which of the following best states the main idea of this passage?

   (1) Guitars are harder to play than harmonicas.
   (2) Guitars and harmonicas are musical instruments.
   (3) Harmonicas can sound like bagpipes.
   (4) Harmonicas are satisfying to play, portable, and cheap compared to guitars.
   (5) Harmonicas are small enough to play anywhere.

2. Which of the following details tells you most about where this story takes place?

   (1) A harmonica is easy to carry.
   (2) Take it out of your hip pocket....
   (3) ...you learn new tricks, new ways to mold the tone...
   (4) ...in the tent door after supper...
   (5) You can buy another for a quarter.

3. What can you infer about the narrator?

   He is

   (1) content and thoughtful
   (2) frustrated and lonely
   (3) lazy and indifferent
   (4) bored and impatient
   (5) quiet and forgiving

Questions 4 through 7 refer to the following article.

HOW CAN YOU BE PREPARED FOR A PET EMERGENCY?

Preparing for a Pet Emergency

Accidents and injuries are the number one cause of death and disability for dogs and cats in their prime. Prevention of injuries is the best course of action,
(5) but if injuries do occur, it's important to be prepared.

Emergency Preparedness Kit

Prepare an emergency kit for your pet and keep it in a container that is
(10) easy to locate and carry. The kit should include basic first aid items, identification and medical information for your pet, a leash, a collar, a crate, a flashlight, a two-week supply of current
(15) medications, canned food for three days, a blanket, a radio, and batteries.

Pet Emergency Hospital

Accidents can occur at very impractical times—such as after 5:00 p.m. when
(20) your vet's office is closed. Know the name and location of the nearest 24-hour pet emergency hospital. Keep the phone number along with other vital numbers in your emergency kit.

(25) *Pet Identification*

There are several ways to identify your pet, the most common being a tag on the pet's collar that has a name and phone number. You can also ask your vet
(30) to implant an identification chip. If there is a disaster (such as a flood or fire), or if your pet is startled by fireworks or thunder, it may run away. Identification could be the saving grace that brings
(35) your pet home safely. Also keep a picture of your pet in your emergency kit for easy access if an emergency arises.

4. What is the main idea of this passage?

   (1) Be prepared for emergencies with your pet.
   (2) Accidents occur at impractical times.
   (3) An emergency kit should be easy to carry.
   (4) There are several ways to identify your pet.
   (5) Disasters can cause pets to run away.

5. Which detail best supports the idea that you should know where the nearest pet emergency hospital is?

   (1) Prevention is the best course of action.
   (2) Your pet may be startled by fireworks or thunder.
   (3) The emergency kit should include extra food and water.
   (4) The vet may be closed when your pet is hurt.
   (5) Identification could bring the pet home.

6. Based on the passage, why is it important to have your pet's photo handy?

   (1) to give it to the vet
   (2) to show it to people if your pet is lost
   (3) to remember your pet in case it dies
   (4) to identify which pet the medications are for
   (5) to use as an ID tag for your pet

7. What is the main idea of the section Emergency Preparedness Kit?

   (1) Keep the kit with you at all times.
   (2) Include first aid items.
   (3) Make sure you have a crate for your pet, plus food for three days.
   (4) Keep at least two-weeks' worth of medications plus a blanket in the kit.
   (5) The kit must be easy to carry and locate and should have important items for a pet emergency.

Sequence of Events

Some questions on the GED Reading Test relate to the **sequence of events,** or the order in which events happen. Some authors do not tell the events of a story in order. As you read, think about the order in which the events took place.

In 1939, Marian Anderson sang for an audience of more than 75,000 at the Lincoln Memorial in Washington, D.C. First Lady Eleanor Roosevelt had arranged for the performance soon after Anderson's request to sing at Constitution Hall was denied because she was African-American. Anderson had first come to the public's attention when she sang in church choirs in Philadelphia. As word of her amazing vocal talent spread, she had been offered many scholarships to study music. As a result of her fame, she toured Europe in 1925 with the New York Philharmonic Orchestra.

1. Of all the performances described in the passage, which came first?

   _____

2. What happened after Anderson's request to sing in Constitution Hall was denied?

   _____

1. The earliest performances mentioned in the paragraph were in church choirs in Philadelphia. 2. Eleanor Roosevelt arranged for her to sing at the Lincoln Memorial.

Use a sequencing chart to order the events in a passage. Use as many boxes as you need.

Order of Events

1	Marian sang in church choirs.
2	She was offered scholarships to study music.
3	1925: She toured Europe with the N.Y. Philharmonic.
4	Her request to sing in Constitution Hall was denied.
5	1939: She sang at the Lincoln Memorial.

To find the sequence of events in a passage, ask yourself:
- Are there clue words or dates to help me put the events in order?
- How do the details of one event lead to the next event?

Have you ever seen a movie that contained a scene in which a character remembered an event from the past? How did you know the scene was from the past?

TIP

Logic or common sense can help you put many events in order. Also look for words like *first*, *then*, and *next* to help you order the events.

UNIT 1 READING

Read the passage and complete the chart with three events. Then answer the questions.

Andrew was surprised to see the shed with the rotting canoe propped against its side. He had been so lost in thought that he hadn't realized he wasn't heading for the Jacobs' farmhouse. Instead, something had pulled him to the deserted boathouse by the river. He cautiously entered the building and struck a match from his pocket. The flickering light revealed a rusted lantern on a shelf. He lit it with a second match. "I knew you'd come," said a deep voice behind him.

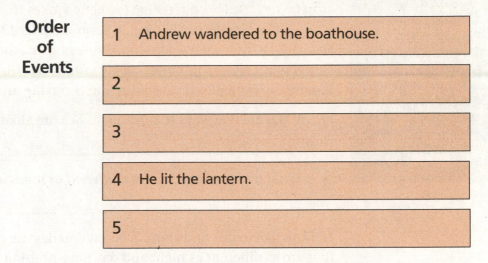

Order of Events

1	Andrew wandered to the boathouse.
2	
3	
4	He lit the lantern.
5	

1. The first sentence says that Andrew was surprised. Based on the passage, what happened before this?

   _____

2. What did Andrew do immediately after he entered the boathouse?

   _____

GED PRACTICE   Choose the **one best answer** to the question.

A doctor placed two cups in front of a nine-month-old baby. Then she put a shiny toy under the first cup. Immediately, the child picked up the cup to find the toy. Next, while the baby was watching, the doctor moved the toy, placing it under the second cup. As the baby reached for the second cup, the doctor clapped her hands four times high in the air as a distraction. The curious baby watched the clapping and then looked for the toy under the first cup. The baby had forgotten that the toy had been moved.

3. The passage describes an experiment a doctor used to test a child's memory. What did the doctor do just before she distracted the child?

   (1) She clapped her hands loudly.
   (2) She placed the toy under the second cup.
   (3) She placed the toy under the first cup.
   (4) She allowed the baby to hold the toy.
   (5) She changed the position of the cups.

SEQUENCE OF EVENTS   Check your answers on page 152.   **23**

Compare/Contrast

On the GED Reading Test, you may read passages that use comparison and contrast. Authors often **compare** people, places, or things to show how they are the same. Passages can also show **contrast**—how people, places, or things are different. As you read this passage, think about how the sisters are similar and different.

TIP

In some passages, one paragraph may be used to compare and one to contrast. Make sure you read the entire passage before you answer questions about comparing and contrasting.

Billie's daughters Bea and Jean believed they were as different as night and day, but they were really two birds from the same nest. Both were non-stop talkers. Bea liked retelling Jay Leno's jokes from the night before, whereas Jean preferred to discuss serious things like the fate of social security. On many occasions, both sisters spent the whole day shopping. Bea generously spent money on gifts for all her friends. Jean enjoyed looking for bargains at yard sales, rarely buying anything.

1. What are two ways that Jean and Bea are alike?

_____

2. What does it mean to be *as different as night and day*?

_____

1. Both like to talk and shop. 2. Night and day are opposites. Two things that are as different as night and day have nothing in common.

A Venn diagram can help you compare and contrast two people, places, or things. Label the circles and write the qualities in the correct circle. If a quality is shared by both, write it in the overlapping space.

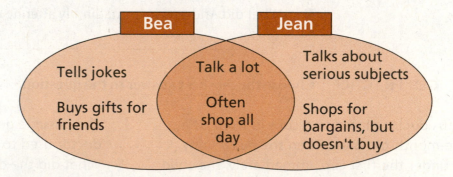

To compare and contrast people, places, and things, ask yourself:
* What are some qualities both share?
* What qualities belong to either one or the other?

Think of two of your favorite desserts. What do they have in common? How are they different?

Read the passage and add at least one more statement to each section of the Venn diagram. Then answer the questions.

The Continental Congress stated only a few requirements for the making of the first American flag. The flag was to have thirteen white stars in a blue field and thirteen stripes, alternating red and white. This simple prescription allowed for much creativity. The first flags had stars with anywhere from four to eight points. These unique flags had additional stripes, symbols, pictures, and colors. In 1914, by executive order, the design of the flag became standard. Now, the size of the flag, its colors, the 50 five-pointed stars, and the thirteen horizontal stripes are uniform.

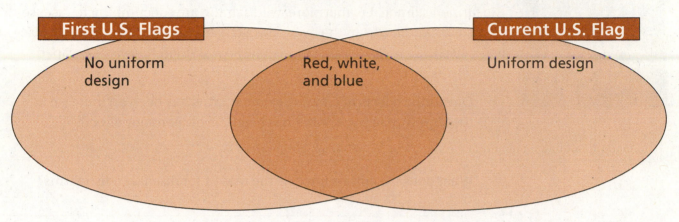

First U.S. Flags

No uniform design

Red, white, and blue

Current U.S. Flag

Uniform design

1. The current design meets the original requirements of the Continental Congress in every way except for one. What is it?

   _____

2. Which description is different from the current flag design?
   a. The first flag of the United States had horizontal red and white stripes.
   b. Some early flags had an eagle stitched in the blue field.

GED PRACTICE Choose the one best answer to the question.

Jeremy went to Sanibel to escape the harsh cold of January in Michigan. The thin barrier island off the coast of Florida was a definite change from the loud, crowded city of Detroit. "Nature matters more here," he thought. From his cabin, he could see mangrove trees and the beach sparkling in the sun. Jeremy took a stroll along the shore. Soon he stooped to retrieve a gleaming object. It was simply a shell, a Venus sunray, but at the moment it seemed more precious than fine gold.

3. The purpose of this paragraph is to contrast which of the following?

   (1) the island and the mangrove trees
   (2) fine gold and the Venus sunray
   (3) the beach and the sunlight
   (4) Detroit and Sanibel
   (5) Jeremy and his feelings about nature

COMPARE/CONTRAST   Check your answers on page 152.   **25**

Cause/Effect

On the GED Reading Test, you will be asked questions about cause-and-effect relationships. A **cause** is an event that makes another event, the **effect,** happen. Read the passage and look for causes and effects.

TIP

Words such as *because* and *since* may signal a cause. Words and phrases like as a *result, therefore,* and *consequently* are often used to signal an effect.

Salmon farms were originally created to relieve the pressure on the wild salmon population. Although these farms have increased the available supply of salmon, they have actually endangered what they were meant to preserve. Many wild salmon are now in danger of starvation. This is because farmers use the wild fish that the wild salmon would eat to feed the farmed salmon. Furthermore, wild salmon are succumbing to diseases that have migrated from the overcrowded fish farms. Wild salmon are also losing territory to the larger, stronger farmed salmon that have escaped from farms into the wild.

1. One of the effects of creating salmon farms has been an increase in the supply of salmon. What has been the other major effect?

_____

2. What does the author imply is the reason for disease in fish farms?

_____

1. The other major effect has been that salmon farms have endangered the population of wild salmon. 2. In the fifth sentence, the author implies that the diseases are caused by overcrowding in the fish farms.

Not all causes and effects are stated directly in order. Also, a cause may have more than one effect and an effect may have several causes. Use a chart to organize your thinking.

CAUSE		EFFECT
Farmers use wild fish to feed farmed salmon.	→	Wild salmon are in danger of running out of food.
Diseases are spreading from fish farms into the wild.	→	Wild salmon are dying from the diseases.
Some larger farmed salmon have escaped into the wild.	→	The stronger farmed salmon have taken over the wild salmon's territories.

To find cause-and-effect relationships, ask yourself:
- What happened in this passage?
- What related event or events caused it to happen?

....

Have you ever caused something to happen? What happened? What did you do to make it happen?

SKILL PRACTICE Read the passage and complete the chart by adding one cause and one effect. Then answer the questions.

A young mother wipes her countertops with the latest antibacterial cleaner. She thinks she is protecting her family from germs, but she is probably making her child's environment more dangerous. Scientists now know that the overuse of antibiotic medicines and cleaners is allowing more powerful strains of bacteria to flourish. Although many germs are killed, those that survive become stronger. In fact, the use of antibiotic cleaners may be counterproductive. When children grow up with normal amounts of bacteria in their homes, their own ability to fight off disease improves.

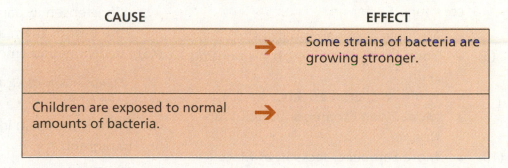

CAUSE		EFFECT
	→	Some strains of bacteria are growing stronger.
Children are exposed to normal amounts of bacteria.	→	

1. What effect do people who use antibacterial cleaners hope to achieve?

_____

2. What actually causes powerful strains of bacteria to flourish?

_____

GED PRACTICE Choose the <u>one best answer</u> to the question.

To: All Employees
From: Westbrook Management

Because of everyone's great efforts, we had strong sales this Christmas season. In spite of a slow economy, we were able to post a 5% increase in sales over last Christmas. The marketing department's suggestion of free shipping on all Internet sales caught customers' attention. Our fine workers in shipping and receiving put in many hours of overtime to make sure that we could fill all of our orders. Everyone contributed to our success and management would like to thank you with the enclosed bonus. Happy New Year to you and your families!

3. According to the memo, what caused the company to be profitable during the Christmas season?

(1) a stronger economy
(2) layoffs and budget cutbacks
(3) a smart marketing promotion and hard work
(4) a 5% increase in profits over the previous Christmas
(5) a New Year's bonus for all employees

Reading Practice 2

Directions: Choose the one best answer to each question.

Questions 1 through 3 refer to the following excerpt from a movie review.

WHAT DOES THE REVIEWER THINK OF THE MOVIE?

Star Wars Episode II: Attack of the Clones contains plenty to cheer hard-core fans. Such as:

- Multiple light-saber battles.
- (5) Yoda finally showing off his fighting skills.
- Faultless special effects.
- More Ewan McGregor as Obi-Wan Kenobi.
- (10) More Samuel L. Jackson as Mace Windu.
- More Boba Fett.
- Less Jar Jar Binks.

(15) Even more heartening to fans who felt let down at the lack of emotional heft in *Episode I: the Phantom Menace,* the new movie makes room for a love story featuring a pair of gorgeous young stars. Jedi-in-training Anakin Skywalker (20) (Hayden Christensen), now 19, has grown into a fine warrior, as well as a bundle of youthful conflicts. He chafes at authority, blurts out rude comments and complains about father figure Obi- (25) Wan Kenobi. ("He always criticizes! He doesn't understand!")

Anakin is also beside himself with excitement at being assigned to protect the lovely galactic senator Padme (30) Amidala (Natalie Portman), whom he met last when he was only 9.

While Obi-Wan flies around the galaxy discovering a secret clone army ostensibly created to protect the peace- (35) loving republic from dangerous separatists, Anakin and Padme fall crazy in love.

The relationship is sketched out, like almost all *Star Wars* relationships, in (40) skimpy terms. Yet the two young actors are so sincere (and so incredibly attractive) that the romance works. Mr. Christensen in particular smolders with the best of them and brings the movie a (45) badly needed emotional wallop.

Margaret A. McGurk, *Love Story Lifts 'Episode II'*

1. What is the main idea of the last paragraph?

   (1) The love relationship is underdeveloped.
   (2) The two actors are very believable.
   (3) The movie has a romance.
   (4) The movie is lousy without the romance.
   (5) The romance helps the movie.

2. How are Episodes I and II similar?

   (1) Both episodes have a love story.
   (2) There are no special effects.
   (3) There is more time spent on good characters.
   (4) The love story is fully developed.
   (5) Anakin and Obi-Wan are in both films.

3. Why does the reviewer quote what Anakin says about Obi-Wan (lines 25–26)?

   To show that

   (1) Obi-Wan is impossible to deal with
   (2) Anakin can be frustrated by Obi-wan
   (3) Anakin is a fine warrior
   (4) the reader should feel sorry for Anakin
   (5) Obi-Wan is well-rounded

Questions 4 through 8 refer to the following excerpt from a novel.

DOES THE MAN KNOW WHERE HE IS GOING?

That morning he had got off the train at a junction stop to get some air and while he had been looking the other way, the train had slid off. He had run
(5) after it but his hat had blown away and he had had to run in the other direction to save the hat. Fortunately, he had carried his duffel bag out with him lest someone should steal something out of
(10) it. He had to wait six hours at the junction stop until the right train came.

When he got to Taulkinham, as soon as he stepped off the train, he began to see signs and lights. PEANUTS, WESTERN
(15) UNION, AJAX, TAXI, HOTEL, CANDY. Most of them were electric and moved up and down or blinked frantically. He walked very slowly, carrying his duffel bag by the neck. His head turned to one
(20) side and then the other, first toward one sign and then another. He walked the length of the station and then he walked back as if he might be going to get on the train again. His face was stern
(25) and determined under the heavy hat. No one observing him would have known that he had no place to go. He walked up and down the crowded waiting room two or three times, but he did not want
(30) to sit on the benches there. He wanted a private place to go to.

Flannery O'Connor, *Wise Blood*

4. What can be inferred about the man?

   (1) He is familiar with big cities.
   (2) He is wealthy.
   (3) He is in a big hurry.
   (4) He is going to visit family.
   (5) He had intended to go to Taulkinham.

5. Which of the following details supports the idea that the man is in a city?

   (1) He waited six hours for the right train.
   (2) He saw signs and lights blinking frantically.
   (3) His face was stern and determined.
   (4) He walked up and down the crowded room.
   (5) He wanted a private place to go.

6. What can be inferred from the line, "No one observing him would have known that he had no place to go?"

   (1) He was an unhappy loner.
   (2) He was forgetful and unfriendly.
   (3) He wore a disguise.
   (4) He was upset about something.
   (5) He appeared as if he had a purpose.

7. What caused the man to miss the train?

   (1) He didn't care much about the train.
   (2) He got off the train for some air.
   (3) He was carrying his duffel bag.
   (4) He was putting his hat back on.
   (5) He was not looking.

8. Which event happened before the man caught the second train?

   (1) He walked slowly with his duffel bag.
   (2) He walked back and forth in the station.
   (3) He looked for a place to be alone.
   (4) He saw signs and lights.
   (5) He waited six hours.

Conclusions

On the GED Reading Test, you will be asked to draw conclusions about the ideas in a passage. A **conclusion** is an idea that follows logically from facts or evidence. Read the passage and draw your own conclusions.

> Although millions of Americans play soccer, the sport has yet to find a large television audience in the United States. With its large field of play and spread out action, a soccer game is difficult to watch on a television screen. Soccer has continuous action, making it difficult for American television networks to schedule commercial breaks. Compared to popular televised sports, soccer is low scoring with less physical contact.

1. What fact supports the conclusion that Americans like soccer?

_____

2. What conclusion can you draw about the future of soccer and American television?

_____

1. The fact that millions of Americans play soccer means that Americans do like the sport. 2. One possible conclusion is that soccer probably won't gain popularity with American audiences because it is difficult to watch on TV and is not as exciting as other sports.

You can use this diagram to organize your thinking. The <u>facts</u> (columns) support the <u>conclusion</u> (roof).

CONCLUSION				
Soccer probably won't become popular with American television audiences.				
The large field is hard to see on TV.	F A C T S	Networks need commercial breaks.	F A C T S	Viewers like high scores and physical contact.

To draw a conclusion, ask yourself:
- What facts are presented in the passage?
- How do these facts work together to support a conclusion?

Have you ever drawn a conclusion and explained it to someone? How did you use facts to support your idea?

Read the passage and add two more facts that can support the conclusion. Then answer the questions.

Alan hugged the cliff wall next to the hiking path. He had agreed to make the short climb to the cave entrance because everyone else in the family was going. "The trail is paved and carefully marked. What's going to happen to you?" his sister teased. Sure the trail was paved and marked, but there was no handrail. Why didn't anyone say there would be no handrail? One little misstep and off the edge he would go. It could happen to anyone. "Get away from the edge!" he wanted to yell, but they were too busy laughing and talking. Didn't anyone else see the danger?

CONCLUSION
Alan's fear is unreasonable.

Alan is hugging the cliff wall.	F A C T S		F A C T S	

1. What fact supports the idea that Alan's family doesn't think they are in danger?

_____

2. How do you think Alan's family members feel about his fears?

_____

GED PRACTICE Choose the one best answer to the question.

Cesar Chavez, the famous union leader, was born in 1927. Although he was born on a farm, his family became migrant farm workers during the Great Depression. He attended 65 elementary schools and never graduated from high school. In 1962, he founded the National Farm Workers Association (NFWA), based in California and the Southwest. The NFWA attracted national attention in 1965 when Chavez led the union in a strike and called for a national boycott of table grapes. To highlight the plight of farm workers, Chavez also fasted for 28 days. The strike and boycott lasted until 1970 and ended with the first major victory for migrant workers in the U.S.

3. Which of the following conclusions can you draw based on the facts from the passage?

(1) Cesar Chavez did not like farm work.
(2) The National Farm Workers Association was founded in 1927.
(3) Chavez's personal leadership played a big role in the union's success.
(4) The strike and boycott did not accomplish their goals.
(5) Farm workers now enjoy the same benefits as other unionized workers.

Author's Purpose

On the GED Reading Test, you may be asked to identify the **author's purpose.** Most of the time, an author writes to inform, persuade, or entertain. The author's choice of supporting facts, words, dialogue, and descriptive details gives clues to his or her purpose. Read this passage to find the author's purpose.

Every year, thousands of cats and dogs are taken to animal shelters because the number of these neglected animals far exceeds the number of available homes. There they sit alone and frightened. It doesn't have to be this way. Spay or neuter pets to prevent another generation of homeless animals. Consider adopting pets from a shelter instead of buying from a breeder or pet store. If we work together, we can spare our animal friends much suffering.

1. What is the author's main purpose? *(inform, persuade, or entertain)*

_____

2. What words and phrases are used to appeal to the reader's emotions?

_____

1. The author wants to persuade the reader to care about homeless animals and take action. 2. The author describes the animals as *neglected, alone, frightened,* and *homeless.*

Organize your thinking with a chart. Think about what the author wants you to feel or do and write the author's purpose in the top box. Use the other boxes to write supporting facts, opinions, key words, and phrases.

Author's Purpose	
To persuade readers to care about homeless animals and take action.	
Supporting Facts and Opinions	**Key Words and Phrases**
There are more animals than there are homes. People can help by spaying and neutering their pets and by adopting animals from shelters.	The animals are described as *neglected, alone, frightened,* and *homeless.*

To find the author's purpose, ask yourself:

● What does the author want me to do, feel, or think?

● What does the author feel or think about the subject?

....

Think of a time when you had to convince someone that you were right. What did you do to persuade the other person?

Read the passage and add to the chart. Then answer the questions.

Our company suffered substantial losses last quarter. To avoid layoffs, we must instigate cost-cutting measures immediately, and we are asking for your cooperation during this difficult time. Too many absent employees hurt our productivity, so we are requesting that all employees give at least one month's notice before using vacation leave. Temporary workers further stretch our budget. Therefore, to reduce our reliance on temporary workers, we ask that all employees schedule any planned absences with their supervisors. Our goal is to have no more than two workers out per department on any given day. Your cooperation is critical in helping us avoid severe budget cuts and possible layoffs.

Author's Purpose	
Supporting Facts and Opinions The company must save money to avoid layoffs.	**Key Words and Phrases** difficult time suffered substantial losses

1. What is the author asking the employees to do?

   _____

2. What words or phrases are used to appeal to the readers' emotions?

   _____

GED PRACTICE **Choose the one best answer to the question.**

Mrs. Oliphant was an energetic third grade teacher. A pair of large glasses with thick lenses hung around her neck on a chain. She held them shyly to her eyes with one hand as she read us *King Arthur and the Knights of the Round Table.* I closed my eyes and her low contralto voice lifted me across a great divide. I was Gareth, the kitchen boy, slaying the mighty Black Knight and then kneeling while Sir Lancelot raised his heavy broadsword to knight me. Then I heard the closing of the book, and gently, so gently, Mrs. Oliphant told us to open our eyes.

3. In this passage, the author describes the childhood experience of being read to by a teacher. Which of these word choices is used to communicate that Mrs. Oliphant respected the children's feelings about the experience?

   (1) energetic
   (2) thick
   (3) shyly
   (4) mighty
   (5) gently

AUTHOR'S PURPOSE

Check your answers on page 153. **33**

Reading Practice 3

Directions: Choose the <u>one best</u> answer to each question.

DOES THIS OLD MAN POSE A DANGER?

<u>Questions 1 through 4</u> refer to the following excerpt from a novel.

     Aragorn looked and beheld a bent
figure moving slowly. It was not far
away. It looked like an old beggar-man,
walking wearily, leaning on a rough
(5) staff. His head was bowed, and he did
not look towards them. In other lands
they would have greeted him with kind
words; but now they stood silent, each
feeling a strange expectancy:
(10) something was approaching that held a
hidden power—or menace.
     Gimli gazed with wide eyes for a
while, as step by step the figure drew
nearer. Then suddenly, unable to
(15) contain himself longer, he burst out:
'Your bow, Legolas! Bend it! Get ready!
It is Saruman. Do not let him speak, or
put a spell upon us! Shoot first!'
     Legolas took his bow and bent it,
(20) slowly and as if some other will resisted
him. He held an arrow loosely in his
hand but did not fit it to the string.
Aragorn stood silent, his face was
watchful and intent.
(25)   'Why are you waiting? What is the
matter with you?' said Gimli in a hissing
whisper.
     'Legolas is right,' said Aragorn
quietly. 'We may not shoot an old man
(30) so, at unawares and unchallenged,
whatever fear or doubt be on us. Watch
and wait!'

J. J. R. Tolkien, *The Two Towers Being the Second Part of The Lord of the Rings*

1. What best explains why Legolas doesn't shoot when he picks up his bow?

   (1) The bow breaks in half.
   (2) He is using the wrong arrows.
   (3) The old man has put a spell on him.
   (4) He isn't sure it's right to shoot the man.
   (5) He wants Aragorn's approval.

2. Why does Aragorn conclude that they should not shoot the man?

   Because the man

   (1) appears harmless
   (2) may put a curse on them
   (3) may be a stranger
   (4) may be able to help them
   (5) is moving too slowly

3. How is Gimli different from Aragorn and Legolas?

   (1) He knows the old man has already cast a spell.
   (2) He would rather be safe than sorry.
   (3) He thinks before he acts.
   (4) He is mean-spirited.
   (5) He has better eyesight.

4. Why does the author include the detail, "It looked like an old beggar-man, walking wearily, leaning on a rough staff"?

   (1) to make it seem like the man couldn't be harmful
   (2) to show that the man was very poor
   (3) to explain exactly how he looked
   (4) to illustrate that he walked slowly
   (5) to show he didn't have a weapon

Questions 5 through 7 refer to the following excerpt from an essay.

HOW SHOULD YOU READ A BOOK?

It is simple enough to say that since books have classes—fiction, biography, poetry—we should separate them and take from each what it is right that
(5) each should give us. Yet few people ask from books what books can give us. Most commonly we come to books with blurred and divided minds, asking of fiction that it shall be true, of poetry
(10) that it shall be false, of biography that it shall be flattering, of history that it shall enforce our own prejudices. If we could banish all such preconceptions when we read, that would be an
(15) admirable beginning. Do not dictate to your author; try to become him. Be his fellow-worker and accomplice. If you hang back, and reserve and criticise at first, you are preventing yourself from
(20) getting the fullest possible value from what you read. But if you open your mind as widely as possible, then signs and hints of almost imperceptible fineness, from the twist and turn of the
(25) first sentences, will bring you into the presence of a human being unlike any other. Steep yourself in this, acquaint yourself with this, and soon you will find that your author is giving you, or
(30) attempting to give you, something far more definite.

Virginia Woolf, "How Should One Read a Book?"

5. Which of the following statements best expresses the main idea of this passage?

   (1) It's important to think of each class of book separately.
   (2) It's a good idea to expect that fiction and poetry are true.
   (3) The reader should learn to think critically, by thinking like the author.
   (4) The reader should follow the twists and turns of a book to get inside the minds of the characters.
   (5) The reader should get rid of any preconceived ideas and be open to what the author has to give.

6. Based on the passage, which of the following conclusions can be made about keeping an open mind?

   (1) It allows the reader to learn more from the author.
   (2) It makes the reader more vulnerable to criticism by friends.
   (3) The author will admire the reader for it.
   (4) The reader must be careful not to twist the author's meaning.
   (5) The reader will read more of all classes of books.

7. Which of the following best explains what the author means by "be his fellow-worker and accomplice"?

   (1) Write your own book.
   (2) Correct the writing as you are reading.
   (3) Believe nothing the writer says.
   (4) Try hard to understand difficult books.
   (5) Join with the author's vision as you read.

Setting

On the GED Reading Test, you may be asked questions about the setting of a passage. The **setting** tells where and when the action of the passage takes place. As you read, try to picture the action. Look for descriptive clues in the passage below that will help you identify the time of day and the place.

The automatic doors swept aside as Linda entered. She squinted in the bright fluorescent light as she walked toward the information desk. "Excuse me. My friend Celia is here. There was a little accident." Linda stopped short. All the attention had shifted to a father carrying a small child. Linda wandered through a door. Perhaps she could find Celia on her own. The treatment rooms were small and smelled of antiseptic. In an empty room, a television was broadcasting a replay of the evening news. Long pleated pink curtains surrounded the occupied beds. A technician carrying a tray of test tubes pushed past her. She'd never find Celia this way.

1. Where is Linda looking for Celia?

_____

2. What detail tells you the action takes place sometime in the middle of the night?

_____

1. Linda is looking for Celia in the emergency room at a hospital. All the clues point to some type of medical building. 2. There is a rerun of the evening news on television.

Use your senses to find clues to the setting. You can organize your thinking with a chart.

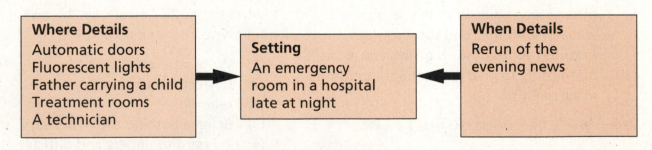

Where Details
Automatic doors
Fluorescent lights
Father carrying a child
Treatment rooms
A technician

Setting
An emergency room in a hospital late at night

When Details
Rerun of the evening news

To find the setting, ask yourself:
- What clues describe the place, time of day, and time of year?
- What words tell how things look and sound?

....

Think of a time when you told a friend about an experience from your childhood. What words did you use to describe the setting?

Read the passage and add where and when details to the chart. Then answer the questions.

Back in those days, NASA scientists weren't sure how astronauts would react to the weightless environment of space, so we became their lab rats. The scientists developed a training program. They started taking the seven of us on rides in the cargo hold of a large Air Force C131 transport. The engines would roar as we climbed in a steep arc, and then just as we went over the top, we felt up to a minute of weightlessness. They wanted to see if we could do simple tasks like talking, reading gauges, flipping switches, and keeping down our breakfasts.

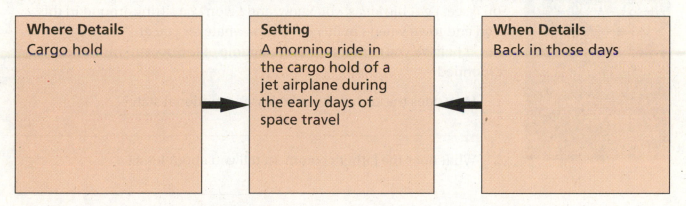

Where Details	Setting	When Details
Cargo hold	A morning ride in the cargo hold of a jet airplane during the early days of space travel	Back in those days

1. What detail suggests that the training program was also an experiment?

   _____

2. Based on details in the passage, riding in the cargo hold was most like which of the following?
   a. going over a hill on a roller coaster
   b. making a sharp turn in a fast car

GED PRACTICE   **Choose the <u>one best answer</u> to the question.**

Millie couldn't see how she was going to get to the front door of the Mirage Beauty Salon without stepping in the tar. Apparently, the city had decided to resurface the street on the same day that she had scheduled a perm. Some big machine was spraying hot oil and sending bits of black grit flying everywhere. A few men stood around with stop signs doing absolutely nothing. When the light changed, she hurried across the street and into the small shop with no sign of any tar on her shoes.

3. Based on the details in the passage, which of the following is the most accurate description of when this event takes place?

The action takes place

(1) during the late evening
(2) during the daytime
(3) on a weekend
(4) during a rainstorm
(5) in the future

Character

On the GED Reading Test, you will be asked questions about fictional characters. A **character** is a person created by an author through description and speech. As you read the passage below, think about what the character is like.

Jesse spun the globe and stopped it quickly by pressing his fingertip, ragged fingernail and all, on the slick metal surface. "That's it. That's where I'll be as soon as I save up enough money." he said defiantly. "Anyplace will be better than here. And I'll start my own company and be my own boss. You'll see. I got big ideas, you know, and I won't be sitting around in this dead end town when I'm fifty or sixty or whatever you are."

"I believe you're pointing at the middle of the ocean." his father responded.

1. How does the author describe Jesse's emotional state?

_____

2. What does the father's comment tell you about Jesse?

_____

1. The passage states that Jesse spoke defiantly. Jesse is likely frustrated and angry. 2. The father's comment suggests that Jesse doesn't really have a plan to leave.

Characters are defined by their physical description, actions, and words, as well as the words and reactions of other characters. You can organize these details on a character chart. (You may not always have something to write in each section.)

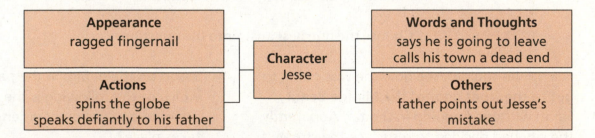

Appearance		Words and Thoughts
ragged fingernail	**Character**	says he is going to leave
	Jesse	calls his town a dead end
Actions		**Others**
spins the globe		father points out Jesse's
speaks defiantly to his father		mistake

To understand a character, ask yourself:
- How do I picture the character?
- Do I know anyone with similar characteristics?

··

Have you ever described your family to a friend? What details did you choose to explain what your family is like?

TIP
On the GED Reading Test, you may be asked to decide how a character would act in a different situation. You must use what you know about the character to make that decision.

Read the passage and add one appearance detail and one action to the chart. Then answer the questions.

Sheila was born under a curse. She was ordinary looking, fairly small but with efficient, perfect posture. Her dull brown hair was never out of place. She had her teeth cleaned every six months, and she ate exactly the recommended number of servings of fruits and vegetables each day. It would be hard to imagine a more perfect person, except Sheila had been cursed. You see, when Sheila met other people, she instantly knew what their biggest faults were. The faults came to her in a flash and it was so very, very hard not to tell them.

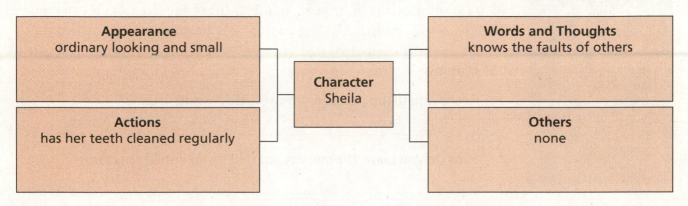

Appearance
ordinary looking and small

Actions
has her teeth cleaned regularly

Character
Sheila

Words and Thoughts
knows the faults of others

Others
none

1. What is Sheila's curse?

_____

2. Which of the following would Sheila be more likely to do at a party?
   a. compliment the hostess on her decorations
   b. tell the hostess how to make better decorations

GED PRACTICE   **Choose the one best answer to the question.**

Elio signed up for a computer class, but he didn't go. Instead, he pecked out a letter, asking for a refund, on an old manual typewriter that he kept under his bed. Elio believed firmly that computers were just a fad. "It's silly to spend so much time learning to do something that won't be around in ten years," he thought. Elio's boss, however, didn't share his opinion. In fact, his boss told him that if he didn't get with the program, Elio's job wouldn't last another ten days. Elio wiped the dust off the typewriter case and slid it back under the bed.

3. Elio doesn't like microwave ovens because he says "nuked food doesn't taste right."

   Based on this information and the details in the passage, which word best describes Elio's attitude toward new technology?

   (1) admiring
   (2) fearful
   (3) disapproving
   (4) disgusted
   (5) interested

Check your answers on page 154.   **39**

Point of View

On the GED Reading Test, you will be asked questions about point of view. Authors tell stories through the eyes, ears, and thoughts of others. How the author chooses to tell the story is the **point of view.** Some stories are told by the main character or by a supporting character. Others are told by an outside narrator. As you read this passage, think about who is telling the story.

My shot to the green looked to be about 150 yards. My partner told me to use a five iron, but I feel more control with a six iron. I took my stance. Then I started talking to myself. "You really need the five iron. If you come up short, you'll dump it in the sand trap." My partner looked down at the ground disapprovingly. Oh, well. I emptied my mind and swung. The ball ended up two feet from the hole.

1. According to the passage, who sees this event?

   _____

2. How do you know the story is not told by an outside narrator?

   _____

1. The event is seen by the golfer and his partner. 2. The pronouns *I, my,* and *me* tell you that the golfer who made the shot is telling the story.

You can organize your ideas in a point-of-view chart. Record who is present, and then examine what happens and how it's described.

Who is present?	A golfer and his partner
What is seen?	A great golf shot, the partner looking down
What is heard?	The golfer's thoughts
Point of view?	The golfer who made the shot

To find the point of view, ask yourself:
- Through whose eyes am I seeing the events of the story?
- Whose side of the story am I learning the most about?

....

Have you and a friend ever had an experience and then shared your points of view? How did your points of view differ?

Read the passage and complete the chart. Then answer the questions.

It would be hard to imagine Abraham Lincoln running for President in today's world. He would make a startling image for the television cameras. Lincoln was a towering six feet, four inches. His body was lean and lanky. He had thick, unruly black hair and thoughtful gray eyes. Lincoln made up for his gawky, rough-hewn looks with a wonderful sense of humor. When an opponent once called him "two-faced" during a debate, Lincoln responded, "If I had another face, do you think I'd wear this one?"

Who is present?	
What is seen?	Lincoln's appearance
What is heard?	Part of the debate, comments about how Lincoln would look on television
Point of view?	

1. This story is told from whose point of view?

   a. Lincoln's   b. an outside narrator's

2. If this story were being told from the opponent's point of view, how would he have described Lincoln?

_____

GED PRACTICE   **Choose the one best answer to the question.**

Warren's shoes were untied again. The eight-year-old boy bent down and carefully wrapped the left lace over the right one, pulled it under and through, and tightened the half knot. Then he began to painstakingly make a loop. Warren's mother hovered over him to protect him from the crowd of passersby. Maybe I should buy him slip-on shoes, she wondered to herself. "Let me help you do the second part," she offered, hoping to hurry the process along, but Warren insisted on doing it himself. She had once read that there were thousands of different ways to tie shoes. She hoped Warren would learn at least one way very soon.

3. Based on the passage, which of the following does the reader know?

   (1) Warren's thoughts and feelings
   (2) how Warren looks to the outside world
   (3) why Warren has trouble tying his shoes
   (4) the mother's thoughts and feelings
   (5) the actions of the people passing by

                              Check your answers on page 155.

Reading Practice 4

Directions: Choose the <u>one best</u> answer to each question.

HOW DOES THE SON FEEL?

<u>Questions 1 through 5</u> refer to the following excerpt from a novel.

> We are on the big dirt field back of my school. He sets his collection book on the ground, and steps up to the plate in his coat and his brown fedora.
> (5) He wears square steel-rimmed spectacles, and his hair (which now I wear) is a wild bush the color and texture of steel wool; and those teeth, which sit all night long in a glass in the
> (10) bathroom smiling at the toilet bowl, now smile out at me, his beloved, his flesh and his blood, the little boy upon whose head no rain shall ever fall. "Okay, Big Shot Ballplayer," he says,
> (15) and grasps my new regulation bat somewhere near the middle—and to my astonishment, with his left hand where his right hand should be. I am suddenly overcome with such sadness: I
> (20) want to tell him, *Hey, your hands are wrong,* but am unable to, for fear I might begin to cry—or he might! "Come on, Big Shot, throw the ball," he calls, and so I do—and of course
> (25) discover that on top of all the other things I am just beginning to suspect about my father, he isn't "King Kong" Charlie Keller either.

Philip Roth, *Portnoy's Complaint*

1. Which of the following describes the tone at the end of the passage?

    (1) sad
    (2) angry
    (3) confused
    (4) resentful
    (5) happy

2. Which of the following best explains why the son doesn't correct his father's hands on the bat?

    (1) He is so surprised he can't speak.
    (2) He feels distressed and decides to let it go.
    (3) He doesn't care about his father very much.
    (4) He wants to win the game himself.
    (5) His dad is left-handed so it's okay.

3. Which of the following best describes the father?

    (1) bored
    (2) enthusiastic
    (3) powerful
    (4) unhappy
    (5) understanding

4. Which of the following is from the father's point of view?

    (1) He wears square steel-rimmed spectacles...
    (2) ...the little boy upon whose head no rain shall ever fall.
    (3) ...those teeth which sit all night long in a glass.
    (4) "Hey, your hands are wrong."
    (5) ...he isn't "King Kong" Charlie Keller either.

5. Which of the following most clearly gives a picture of the setting of the story?

    (1) ...back of my school.
    (2) ...steps up to the plate in his coat...
    (3) ...square steel-rimmed spectacles...
    (4) ...grasps my new regulation bat...
    (5) ...his left hand where his right hand should be.

Questions 6 through 8 refer to the following excerpt from a review.

DOES THE REVIEWER LIKE THE FILM?

The inspired casting of Tobey Maguire and the filmmakers' intelligent fidelity to the most appealing aspects of the original Marvel Comics character
(5) ensure that "Spider-Man" is a surprisingly charming and even witty match for the best of Hollywood's comic-book adaptations.

Director Sam Raimi and screenwriter
(10) David Koepp take the risk of letting a bittersweet teen romance loom almost as large in the story line as the lead character's crime-fighting struggles— and it pays off.

(15) There are plenty of corny moments, but the level of camp is never allowed to overwhelm either the romance or the adventure.

And with its alienated teenage hero,
(20) there are times when "Spider-Man" seems to aspire to the profound darkness of the Frank Miller graphic novels that formed the basis of Tim Burton's "Batman."

(25) Orphan Peter Parker (Maguire) is a high school science geek with an unrequited crush on Mary Jane Watson (Kirsten Dunst), the popular but good-hearted beauty who lives—where
(30) else?—next door.

During a school field trip, Peter is bitten by a genetically-engineered super-spider. (Back in 1962 when the original character was created by Stan
(35) Lee and Steve Ditko, the scientific bogey was radiation.)

The next day he wakes up with, among other things, better vision, a muscular physique and a sixth "spider
(40) sense" that warns him of imminent danger.

Remarkably unsurprised by Peter's victory against the class bully in a school fight, Uncle Ben (Cliff Robertson) warns
(45) Peter that "with great power comes great responsibility."

But it takes a tragic error of judgment before Peter even begins to understand what this warning means—
(50) and embarks on a career as an acrobatic crimefighter, swinging between the skyscrapers.

Jonathan Foreman, "Marvel-ous" *New York Post*

6. Which of the following statements best reflects the reviewer's point of view?

This movie is

(1) corny and predictable
(2) silly and romantic
(3) complex and interesting
(4) exciting and frightening
(5) uninspired and boring

7. Which of the following can you infer based on the statement, "intelligent fidelity to the most appealing aspects of the original" (lines 2–4)?

The movie is

(1) exactly like the original comic book
(2) like the comic book in some ways
(3) written for an intelligent audience
(4) more appealing than the comic book
(5) an exploration of the comic's development

8. According to lines 31–41, what created Peter's superpowers in the movie?

(1) a school field trip
(2) a spider bite
(3) a bogeyman
(4) radiation
(5) his muscular physique

     Check your answers on page 155.

Application

Application is an important thinking skill because it allows you to use information you learn by applying it in a new context or situation. On the GED Reading Test, you will be asked to read a passage and then apply the information to a new situation that is stated in a question. Read the short passage below. Then answer the application questions based on it.

Conflict is the foundation for an interesting story. It makes something happen. Generally, conflict in a fictional work is one of four types: *man versus man, man versus nature, man versus society,* and *man versus self.* In each type, a main character is pitted against an opponent. The events of the story deal with how the main character resolves the conflict, whether in victory or defeat.

1. In the movies, famed detective Sherlock Holmes is often challenged by the evil Professor Moriarty, once a math tutor of Holmes. Which type of conflict is this?

   _____

2. In the book *1984* by George Orwell, the main character strives to maintain his freedom from the government's Thought Police. Which type of conflict is this?

   _____

1. Since Sherlock Holmes battles another person, the conflict is *man versus man*. 2. The government represents society, so this conflict is *man versus society*.

For the GED, read the question to learn what the new situation is. Then apply the information you learned from the reading passage to answer the question. You can organize your thinking in an application chart.

New Situation	Given Information
Holmes against Moriarty	man vs. man
main character against Thought Police	man vs. society

To apply information, ask yourself:
- What is the new situation presented in the question?

- How does the given information apply to the new situation?

Have you ever used what you already knew to solve a problem? How did you apply your knowledge to the problem?

Read the company policy and the new situation that is stated in each question. Then complete the chart and answer the questions.

New Flex-Time Policies: Managers may allow employees to alter their schedules to meet family needs when these requirements are met: 1) employees work a 40-hour week, 2) costs to the company do not increase, and 3) each office or operation is covered during normal business hours.

New Situation	Given Information

Walter
  OK
  OK
  OK
	Company Policy
	  1. 40-hour work week
	  2. no increased costs
	  3. office covered

Sue	Company Policy

1. The company operates two shifts—7 a.m. to 3:30 p.m. and 3 p.m. to 10:30 p.m. Walter Ford's wife is going back to work, and he has to get his son off to school. Walter answers customer complaint letters. He asks if he can come in from 9 a.m. to 5:30 p.m. Is this within the scope of the new policies? Why or why not?

_____

2. Sue Garcia is the only employee in the employee benefits department, which operates from 9 a.m. to 5 p.m., who is accessible to both shifts. She needs to take care of her elderly mother and assures you that she can get her work done between 6:30 a.m. and 3:00 p.m. Is this within the scope of the new policies? Why or why not?

_____

GED PRACTICE Choose the one best answer to the question.

Serious head injuries can result in any sport where the participants are traveling at a high rate of speed. Most states require helmets for cycling, but few have mandated the use of helmets for skateboarding, skiing, and snowboarding. To be effective, a helmet must fit properly and guard against the particular dangers of a sport. For example, a ski helmet must cover more of the head than a bicycle helmet. It is designed to protect against collisions with tree branches and the sharp edges of a ski.

3. An athlete asks if a ski helmet would be a good choice for hockey. Which response best applies the ideas in the passage?

(1) No, it is not designed for hockey.
(2) No, it covers too much of the head.
(3) Yes, because both are winter sports.
(4) Yes, if it fits properly.
(5) Yes, all helmets are basically alike.

Synthesis

You synthesize information when you 1) put together several ideas from across a passage or 2) use additional information that is presented in a question and combine it with ideas in the passage. Try the second type of synthesis skill with the passage and the first question below.

TIP

Some GED questions may provide additional information about the passage or the author. Make sure your answer choice is supported by <u>both</u> the passage and the new information.

We were eating breakfast when we heard a rushing sound by the back door. Startled, we looked out the window. The old elm planted by my grandfather had fallen, stopping inches before our house. The tree was old and it could have fallen at any time. Our children played outside under that tree nearly every day of their young lives. I believe the tree chose to fall in the early morning to spare us all.

1. The author believes that animals have a spirit and that they can think and feel. What suggests that the author has the same belief about trees?

_____

2. What ideas did you put together to understand the author's beliefs?

_____

1. The author believes the tree chose when to fall. 2. The author thinks the tree decided when to fall. The author also believes that animals have thoughts and feelings. Therefore, the author thinks that both animals and trees have thoughts and feelings.

Organize your ideas in a synthesis chart. Record the main idea from each source and then combine them to create a new main idea.

Passage Main Idea	Idea with Question
The author thinks that the tree decided when to fall.	The author believes that animals have thoughts and feelings.

Synthesized Idea
The author believes that animals and trees have thoughts and feelings and can care about people.

To synthesize information, ask yourself:
* Across a passage – What does the information have in common?
* If additional information is given in a question – How does this relate to a key idea in the passage?

Have you ever determined how a friend felt by listening to clues in a conversation?

Read the passage and answer the questions below. Then add the ideas to the chart.

President John F. Kennedy's inaugural address has been praised as one of the best public speeches ever delivered. However, President Kennedy did not write the speech himself. Kennedy gave his speechwriter, Ted Sorenson, clear instructions—keep it short, focus on foreign affairs, set a tone for a new era, and don't attack other politicians.

Passage Main Idea	Idea with Question
President Kennedy asked his speechwriter, Ted Sorensen, to write his inaugural address.	

Synthesized Idea

1. Kennedy asked Sorensen to study Lincoln's Gettysburg Address for its "secrets" of success. Why do you think Kennedy asked him to do that?

_____

_____

2. What do you think Sorensen did with that information?

_____

GED PRACTICE **Choose the _one best answer_ to the question.**

Russ had been driving all night in the rain. The red taillights of the cars ahead swam in the glare of the wet windshield. Russ sat up straighter and hunched forward against the steering wheel to stretch out his lower back. The green road signs were impossible to read until he was right up on them. The rain, the windshield wipers, the wet tires on the pavement—the sounds of the night were hypnotic. Russ knew he should check into a motel and sleep for a few hours, but he was running out of time and Jamie was counting on him. The rain was getting heavier now. He turned the radio up even louder and began to sing at the top of his lungs.

3. The author of this passage once drove from Chicago to Los Angeles without stopping, a feat that he often bragged about to his friends.

The author would probably use which of the following words to describe Russ?

(1) foolish
(2) determined
(3) likable
(4) loyal
(5) overconfident

Reading Practice 5

Directions: Choose the <u>one best</u> answer to each question.

WHAT DOES THE REVIEWER THINK OF THE MOVIE?

Questions 1 and 2 refer to the following excerpt from a movie review.

A cynic might think old Elmore has revenge on his mind, getting back at what Hollywood has done to a few of his novels by writing this acidic, get-
(5) them-laughing-then-punch-them-in-the-gut, splendidly entertaining crime tale. Its moral seems to be that gangsters are a lot like the people who make movies, except crooks are more efficient and
(10) have a deeper sense of honor.

Leonard's protagonist, Chili Palmer, is an easy-going kind of loan shark, in semiretirement in Florida. But then one of his clients skips off to Las Vegas still
(15) owing him, so Chili dutifully takes off after him. It's not long before Palmer is in Los Angeles, hooking up with a has-been horror movie producer, Harry Zimm, a former B-movie actress, Karen
(20) Flores, and a current star, Michael Weir. Soon Chili is deciding he knows enough—which isn't all that much—to get into the filmmaking business.

It wouldn't be a Leonard novel
(25) without colorful villains, and this one has Ray Bones, an old enemy who has become Chili's boss in the Florida hierarchy, and Bo Catlett, a slick-dressing Angeleno who with his pal
(30) Ronnie is a jack-of-all-crimes, including murder.

In this company Chili comes off as a relatively nice guy, and one who knows how to use his expertise. "'What's the
(35) guy gonna do, Catlett, take a swing at me?'" he says to Harry. "'He might've

wanted to, but he had to consider first, who is this guy? He don't know me. All he knows is I'm looking at him like if he
(40) wants to try me I'll...take him apart. Does he wanta go for it, get his suit messed up? I mean even if he's good he can see it would be work.'"

"'He could've had a gun," Harry
(45) said.'"

"'It wasn't a gun kind of situation.'"

Harry himself is on the hard-bitten side, recalling one unpleasant literary agent he had dealt with: "I asked him
(50) one time what type of writing brought the most money and the agent says, 'Ransom notes.'"

Things fall into place too easily for Chili at times, but Leonard compensates
(55) with nice twists, snappy action scenes and more than one blood-drawing zinger.

Ralph Novak, 'Get Shorty' by Elmore Leonard

1. Which of the following words best describes the tone of this review?

   (1) angry
   (2) sympathetic
   (3) humorous
   (4) serious
   (5) worried

2. What type of books does this reviewer probably prefer?

   (1) easy-going romance novels
   (2) lively adventure books
   (3) gourmet cookbooks
   (4) detailed biographies
   (5) classic English novels

Questions 3 through 6 refer to the following excerpt from a novel.

HOW DO THE CHARACTERS FEEL?

Rainwater held on to pine needles
for dear life and Beloved could not take
her eyes off Sethe. Stooping to shake
the damper, or snapping sticks for
(5)   kindlin, Sethe was licked, tasted, eaten
by Beloved's eyes. Like a familiar, she
hovered, never leaving the room Sethe
was in unless required and told to. She
rose early in the dark to be there,
(10) waiting, in the kitchen when Sethe
came down to make fast bread before
she left for work. In lamplight, and over
the flames of the cooking stove, their
two shadows clashed and crossed on
(15) the ceiling like black swords. She was
in the window at two when Sethe
returned, or the doorway; then the
porch, its steps, the path, the road, till
finally, surrendering to the habit,
(20) Beloved began inching down Bluestone
Road further and further each day to
meet Sethe and walk her back to 124.
It was as though every afternoon she
doubted anew the older woman's return.
(25)   Sethe was flattered by Beloved's
open, quiet devotion. The same
adoration from her daughter (had it
been forthcoming) would have
annoyed her; made her chill at the
(30) thought of having raised a ridiculously
dependent child. But the company of
this sweet, if peculiar, guest pleased her
the way a zealot pleases his teacher.

Toni Morrison, *Beloved*

3. What is the relationship between Sethe and Beloved?

   (1) Sethe is Beloved's teacher.
   (2) Sethe is Beloved's child.
   (3) Beloved is Sethe's guest.
   (4) Beloved is Sethe's teacher.
   (5) Beloved is Sethe's cook.

4. If Beloved were reading a book that she liked, which of the following would she most likely do?

   (1) learn more about the author
   (2) pretend she was the main character
   (3) lend the book to a good friend
   (4) read the book several times
   (5) talk about it a lot with friends

5. Why does the author describe Beloved's encounters with Sethe in so much detail?

   To show

   (1) the extent of Beloved's feelings for Sethe
   (2) how little time Beloved spends working
   (3) how annoying Beloved's behavior is
   (4) how much energy Beloved has
   (5) that Beloved makes friends easily

6. Sethe is a former slave, whose master wanted her children to become enslaved. Sethe had killed one of her children rather than seeing that happen.

   Based on the information above and in the excerpt, which of following best describes Sethe?

   (1) grumpy, with a strong will
   (2) compassionate, with a painful history
   (3) wishy-washy, with a gentle temperament
   (4) self-important, with a stubborn streak
   (5) nervous, with a cold disposition

Mini-Test • Unit 1

This is a 15-minute practice test. After 15 minutes, mark the last number you finished. Then complete the test and check your answers. If most of your answers were correct but you did not finish, try to work faster next time.

Directions: Choose the <u>one best</u> answer to each question.

Questions 1 through 6 refer to the following excerpt from a music review.

DID THE REVIEWER ENJOY THIS CONCERT?

One can only imagine the shiver that ran down hit-maker Clive Davis' spine when he came across Keys, now 21, when she was still a teenager. Musically

(5) gifted as both a vocalist and pianist, with songwriting skills beyond her years, physically stunning and oozing charisma, a seamless fusion of classic soul and streetwise sass, Keys is the total

(10) package, a record executive's dream.

In June 2001, Keys' debut disc, "Songs in A Minor," arrived on the charts at No. 1 via Davis' J Records and much marketing fanfare.

(15) Both the "TRL" crowd and their parents couldn't seem to get enough of Keys' lush songs of heartbreak and hope, such as the ubiquitous "Fallin'." In February, the native New Yorker took home an armload

(20) of Grammys for the album.

Fortunately for the Marcus crowd, Keys wears all that commercial and critical success as easily as her signature sequined fedoras.

(25) Emerging onto a set made to look like a Manhattan block party, Keys led her band through "Rock Wit U," stretching the celebratory anthem into a loose jam. The free-flowing opener was a sign of things

(30) to come—throughout her 100-minute set, Keys blended several of her songs into medleys and tossed in covers that ranged from The Jackson 5's "ABC" to a funked-up "Light My Fire."

(35) With only one album to her credit, Keys smartly made the most of her 13-piece band's formidable musicianship. Besides the frequent jams—an instrumental buildup to the encore "Fallin'" seemed

(40) almost as long as the song itself—the show was bulked up with some Janet Jackson-style dance numbers and a lengthy musical "showdown" pitting Keys' DJ, DJ Iroc, and rapper Freak Nasty

(45) against the rest of her band while Keys changed costumes.

While the powerful anthem "A Woman's Worth" and a playful cover of Prince's "How Come U Don't Call Me Anymore"

(50) were among the biggest crowd-pleasers, the evening's arguable highlight came when Keys was seated alone onstage with just her piano in front of a starry backdrop.

(55) Armed with only her clarion-clear, soulful voice and dextrous fingers, Keys let loose on a medley that included "Butterflyz" and "Caged Bird," her artistry adding an exclamation point to the

(60) statement that she has arrived.

Gemma Tarlach, "Keys Blends Hits with Covers; Jams," *Milwaukee Journal Sentinel*

1. Which of the following best expresses the main idea of this review?

   (1) The rap music was overdone, but the band was great.
   (2) Keys had so few songs that she needed the band as filler.
   (3) The instrumentals were too long even though the band was good.
   (4) Keys is a multi-talented new artist who puts on a great show.
   (5) The band and DJ were great during a long costume change.

2. Which of the following statements about music company executives is implied by the text.

   Music company executives

   (1) are not as important as the performers
   (2) always find hit artists through hard work
   (3) interfere with a performer's creative expression
   (4) can make any halfway talented artist successful
   (5) sometimes find great artists through sheer luck

3. What was most likely the setting for the performance?

   (1) a small, intimate club
   (2) a major recording studio
   (3) the Grammy awards
   (4) a large concert hall
   (5) a high school auditorium

4. How would the reviewer most likely feel about a two-hour concert by a singer-songwriter who also played guitar?

   The reviewer would be

   (1) happy that there wasn't more variety
   (2) impressed if the person were talented
   (3) irritated that the concert was so long
   (4) overjoyed that there was no DJ or rap music
   (5) angry that it wasn't a country music concert

5. Which of the following best describes the tone of this review?

   (1) snobbish
   (2) passionate
   (3) hostile
   (4) sympathetic
   (5) neutral

6. According to the reviewer, how does Keys handle her success?

   She is

   (1) excited about it
   (2) nervous about it
   (3) at ease with it
   (4) embarrassed about it
   (5) confused by it

DOES KUNTA LIKE TO ANSWER QUESTIONS?

Every time he and his brother would be walking somewhere by themselves, Kunta would imagine that he was taking Lamin on some journey, as men sometimes did
(5) with their sons. Now, somehow, Kunta felt a special responsibility to act older, with Lamin looking up to him as a source of knowledge. Walking alongside, Lamin would ply Kunta with a steady stream of
(10) questions.

"What's the world like?"

"Well," said Kunta, "no man or canoes ever journeyed so far. And no one knows all there is to know about it."

(15) "What do you learn from the arafang?"

Kunta recited the first verses of the Koran in Arabic and then said, "Now you try." But when Lamin tried, he got badly confused—as Kunta had known he
(20) would—and Kunta said paternally, "It takes time."

"Why does no one harm owls?"

"Because all our dead ancestors' spirits are in owls." Then he told Lamin
(25) something of their late Grandma Yaisa. "You were just a baby, and cannot remember her."

"What's that bird in the tree?"

"A hawk."

(30) "What does he eat?"

"Mice and other birds and things."

"Oh."

Kunta had never realized how much he knew—but now and then Lamin asked
(35) something of which Kunta knew nothing at all.

"Is the sun on fire?" Or: "Why doesn't our father sleep with us?"

At such times, Kunta would usually
(40) grunt, then stop talking—as Omoro did when he tired of so many of Kunta's questions. Then Lamin would say no more, since Mandinka home training taught that one never talked to another
(45) who did not want to talk. Sometimes Kunta would act as if he had gone into deep private thought. Lamin would sit silently nearby, and when Kunta rose, so would he. And sometimes, when Kunta didn't
(50) know the answer to a question, he would quickly do something to change the subject.

Alex Haley, *Roots*

7. Who is telling the story?

(1) Kunta
(2) Lamin
(3) Grandma Yaisa
(4) Omoro
(5) an outside narrator

8. Why does Kunta grunt or change the subject when he does not know the answer to a question?

(1) He is tired of the conversation.
(2) He wishes his father were there to answer.
(3) He finds Lamin's questions annoying.
(4) He doesn't want Lamin to realize that he doesn't know the answer.
(5) He is deep in thought and doesn't want to be interrupted.

9. In what way are Kunta and Lamin similar?

(1) They are both very knowledgeable.
(2) They both have difficulty reciting the Koran.
(3) They both understand a lot about nature.
(4) They both ask a lot of questions.
(5) They both have fond memories of Yaisa.

10. Based on information in the last paragraph, what would Kunta probably do if Lamin suddenly became quiet?

He would probably

(1) grunt and ask him a question
(2) teach him about animals
(3) stop talking to him
(4) change the subject
(5) get angry with him

11. Which of the following is most likely Lamin's opinion of Kunta?

(1) He resents Kunta.
(2) He is confused by Kunta.
(3) He feels Kunta is his father.
(4) He wants to be like Kunta.
(5) He feels intimidated by Kunta.

Check your answers on pages 156–157.

Unit 2

Social Studies

The GED Social Studies Test requires you to use your critical thinking skills to answer questions about topics in U.S. and world history, geography, economics, and civics and government. The questions may be based on written passages or various kinds of graphics, such as photographs, maps, graphs, and political cartoons.

Write one way that you use maps to make everyday decisions.

_____

Thinking About Social Studies

You may not realize how often you think about social studies in your everyday life. Think about your recent activities.

Check the box for each activity you did.

- ☐ Did you follow the sequence of events in a movie or television show based on a historical event?
- ☐ Did you think about the causes or effects of an international conflict?
- ☐ Did you use a map to plan a trip or give directions?
- ☐ Did you compare candidates and their views before voting in an election?
- ☐ Did you evaluate whether you had enough information to make an important decision?
- ☐ Did you agree or disagree with opinions voiced in the news?

Write some other activities that involve social studies topics.

_____

_____

_____

Previewing the Unit

In this unit, you will learn:

- how to use thinking skills to understand social studies material

- how to interpret and use the information in photographs, maps, graphs, and political cartoons

- why it is important to evaluate data and ideas when reading social studies material

Lesson 14	Restate/Summarize	Lesson 22	Predict Outcomes
Lesson 15	Implication	Lesson 23	Application
Lesson 16	Graphic Skill: Photographs	Lesson 24	Graphic Skill: Bar Graphs and Line Graphs
Lesson 17	Sequence of Events		
Lesson 18	Cause/Effect	Lesson 25	Fact and Opinion
Lesson 19	Compare/Contrast	Lesson 26	Values and Beliefs
Lesson 20	Graphic Skill: Maps	Lesson 27	Graphic Skill: Political Cartoons
Lesson 21	Adequacy of Data		

Restate/Summarize

On the GED Social Studies Test, you will see questions that ask you to recognize a restatement or summary. A **restatement** or **summary** must retell an idea in fewer words, including only the most important points. As you read the passage below, think about the most important points.

Before the Civil War, most women worked in the home. Some were teachers or nurses, but few held positions outside the household. However, during the war, women took on increasingly crucial roles. When men went to war, women took over their jobs. They worked in mills and munitions plants and ran farms and plantations. Many raised money and distributed supplies. Others served as army scouts and spies. Thousands nursed wounded soldiers. As many as 400 women actually disguised themselves as men, enlisted, and served in battle.

TIP
A summary is brief and restates only the most important points of a passage. A good summary includes the main idea and important details that support the main idea.

1. Summarize in a sentence the most important point of this passage.

_____

2. Restate the last sentence of the passage in your own words.

_____

1. The main point of the passage is that during the Civil War, women took over jobs normally held by men and helped with the war effort. 2. The last sentence could be restated like this: Hundreds of women pretended to be men in order to fight in the war.

To understand restatement and summary, you can put the important ideas in your own words in a chart like the one below.

Important Information
TOPIC: Women's jobs during the Civil War
When men went to war, women filled their jobs. Women worked in industry and business. Women raised money, distributed supplies, and were scouts, spies, and nurses. Hundreds of women even dressed as men and fought in the war.

To summarize or restate a passage, ask yourself:
- What is this passage mainly about?
- What are the most important points or ideas in this passage?

Have you ever summarized a news report for another person? What are some other times when you have summarized or restated something?

SKILL PRACTICE   **Read the passage and add the topic and three important ideas to the chart. Then answer the questions.**

Products manufactured from soybeans include food for people and animals, fertilizer, and oil. Soybeans, valued for their protein content, are native to China, where they have been grown for over 4,000 years. Soybeans were first brought to North America in 1880. They are now grown around the world, but the United States produces more than half of the world's soybeans. Japan and Korea also produce a large portion of the global soybean crop. In recent years, soybean production has increased in South America and in developing African countries.

Important Information
TOPIC:
Made into food, fertilizer, and oil; high protein content Grown in China for over 4,000 years

1. Summarize the passage.

   _____

   _____

2. Summarize the role of the United States in the world soybean market.

   _____

   _____

GED PRACTICE   **Choose the one best answer to the question.**

Article II in the Constitution describes the qualifications needed to be president of the United States. In order to be president, a person must be a natural-born citizen of the United States and must be at least 35-years old. The person must also have been a resident within the United States for no fewer than 14 years prior to the election.

Requirements for voters are less strict. Voters must be American citizens at least 18 years old. Some states have other limits, such as 30-day residency requirements.

3. Which of the following restates the qualifications someone must meet to run for president of the United States?

   (1) citizenship and American residency
   (2) no criminal record, 18 years of age
   (3) natural-born citizen, 35 years of age, 14 years of American residency
   (4) 30 days of American residency, 35 years of age, citizenship
   (5) natural-born citizen, 18 years of age, 14 years of American residency

Implication

On the GED Social Studies Test, you will have to identify information that is implied, or not directly stated. Information that is suggested or hinted at is an **implication.** To understand implications, you need to combine the information given in a passage with what you already know. As you read the passage below, think about what information is implied.

Many events in the American colonies added to the colonists' resentment of British rule. One crucial event occurred in Boston on March 5, 1770. A group of men and boys began to taunt some British soldiers. As the angry mob grew, some threw snowballs at the soldiers. Eventually, the nervous soldiers fired into the crowd, and several colonists were killed. Samuel Adams, a revolutionary, accused the soldiers of murder. In spite of his own politics, Samuel's cousin John Adams represented the British soldiers at trial, arguing that the mob was to blame.

TIP

For implication questions, first rule out answers that are not supported by evidence in the passage. Then decide which of the remaining choices is reasonable.

1. Why did Sam Adams accuse the soldiers of murder?

     _____

2. What were John Adams' views about British rule of the colonies?

     _____

1. The passage suggests that, as a revolutionary, Sam Adams hoped to encourage resentment of British rule. 2. The phrase "in spite of his own politics" implies that John Adams disagreed with British rule.

To understand implications, organize your ideas in a chart. Write information stated in the passage in the first column, what you already know in the second column, and implications in the third column.

Stated Information	What I Already Know	Implication
Sam Adams was a revolutionary.	Revolutionaries were against British rule.	Sam Adams hoped to encourage resentment of British rule.
In spite of his own politics, John Adams represented the soldiers.	"In spite of" suggests doing the opposite.	John Adams was against British rule.

To identify implied ideas, ask yourself:
- What information or evidence is given in the passage? What do I already know?
- How can I combine this information to see what is implied?

....

Have you ever had a conversation in which someone implied something but didn't say it directly? How did you know what the person really meant?

Read the passage, complete the chart, and answer the questions.

Many people collect postage stamps. Some people do this for enjoyment. For others, collecting is more serious. Some stamp collectors possess fortunes in tiny bits of colorful, glue-backed paper.

Old stamps are difficult to find because, as time passes, most stamps are used and thrown away, or are damaged or lost. However, one of the oldest postage stamps is a one-cent stamp that was issued in Guyana (then British Guiana) in 1856. Today the stamp is worth over $900,000.

Stated Information	What I Already Know	Implication
As time passes, most stamps are used and thrown away, or are damaged or lost.	Discard, damage, and loss decrease supply.	
One of the oldest postage stamps is a stamp issued in British Guiana in 1856. It is worth over $900,000.	Old items are often rare and valuable.	

1. How common are old stamps? Why?

_____

2. Why does the stamp from Guyana have such a high value?

_____

GED PRACTICE   **Choose the one best answer to the question.**

The Great Pyramids of Egypt were built over 4,500 years ago as royal tombs. The largest is made of more than two million stones. Here is one theory of how the pyramids were built.

First, workers ran water over the area to wash it clean of debris and to smooth the surface of the ground. Large teams of men dragged the first layer of stones into place, one at a time, using ropes and primitive sleds. Then a ramp was built around the edge of the first level for transporting the second layer of stones. As each layer was put into place, workers added another ramp.

3. Based on the information in the passage, what would be the best description of the stones used to construct the Great Pyramids?

(1) light and manageable
(2) polished and smooth
(3) small and gold-covered
(4) extremely large and heavy
(5) square and brick-sized

IMPLICATION   Check your answers on page 158.   **59**

Photographs

Photographs are images of people, places, things, and events that have been captured by a camera and printed. The GED Social Studies Test includes questions about photographs. Read the information and look at the photograph below. Then answer the questions.

Below is a photograph of a poster. The poster was produced by the Government Printing Office for the War Manpower Commission. The poster was created in 1943, during World War II.

TIP

When you look at photographs of people, look at facial expressions and body language. Try to determine how they feel about the things happening around them.

1. What does the poster show?

_____

_____

2. What was the purpose of this poster?

_____

_____

1. The poster shows two men working on an airplane. There is an American flag in the background and at the bottom is a patriotic slogan.
2. The purpose of this poster was to encourage all Americans to participate in the war effort. It was also to encourage cooperation between Americans.

To interpret a photograph, ask yourself:
* What is happening in the picture?

* What information does this photo provide?

....

Think about a photograph you have seen that impressed you. What did you learn from it? How did it make you feel?

1. What is taking place in the photograph?

   _____

2. What is the mood of the people in the photograph?

   _____

3. What can you conclude from this photograph about the rights of women in U.S. society in the early 1900s?

   _____

GED PRACTICE   Choose the **one best answer** to the question.

4. What can you infer from this photograph taken around 1900?

   (1) Photographs were a popular art form.
   (2) It was taken in a city with a large number of immigrants.
   (3) Photography was recently invented.
   (4) It was taken in a country other than the United States.
   (5) It was taken during wartime.

GRAPHIC SKILL: PHOTOGRAPHS

Social Studies Skills Practice 1

Directions: Choose the <u>one best answer</u> to each question.

<u>Questions 1 and 2</u> refer to the following photograph.

This photograph was taken at a North Carolina cotton mill in 1908.

1. What can you infer from this photograph?

   (1) The cotton mill was owned by children.
   (2) In 1908, young children worked in factories.
   (3) In the early 1900s, children were healthier than they are now.
   (4) The cotton mill was well-run.
   (5) The man in the back row was the children's father.

2. What title could you give the photograph to best summarize its topic?

   (1) Child Labor in 1908
   (2) A Strike at a Cotton Mill
   (3) Children at Play in 1908
   (4) A Typical Turn-of-the-Century Family
   (5) Taking the Children to Work

<u>Questions 3 and 4</u> refer to the following information.

The Silk Road connected China in the East with locations in the West. Its use began as early as 200 BC. One end of the route was in what is now western Iran. It divided into branches and circled the northern and southern borders of the Takla Makan Desert. The branches rejoined at Tun-huang in northwest China. The Silk Road was not only a route for commerce, but also a means for social and cultural trade. For centuries, travelers shared political, social, artistic, and religious customs. When a sea passage was opened between Europe and India in the 15th century, use of the Silk Road greatly declined.

3. Which of the following best summarizes the main idea of this passage?

   (1) The Silk Road ran between western Iran and northwest China.
   (2) The Silk Road was an ancient trade route that connected China and the West.
   (3) The Silk Road was a route for commerce.
   (4) Use of the Silk Road began to decline in the 15th century.
   (5) Cultural beliefs and customs were shared along the Silk Road.

4. What is implied in the final sentence?

   The sentences implies that in the 15th century

   (1) many Europeans visited India
   (2) the Silk Road was destroyed
   (3) boats were invented
   (4) China stopped trading with the West
   (5) travelers preferred using sea routes

Question 5 refers to the following photograph.

This photograph shows a 1937 poster created by the Resettlement Administration. The Administration, created in 1935, worked to rescue farmers whose farms had been destroyed by severe drought. During the 1930s, severe drought caused devastating dust storms that destroyed land throughout the Great Plains. This region was known as the Dust Bowl. The poster shows a farmer whose land has suffered from years of drought. At the bottom is a list of some of the objectives of the Resettlement Administration.

YEARS OF DUST

RESETTLEMENT ADMINISTRATION
Rescues Victims
Restores Land to Proper Use

5. What does the poster imply?

    (1) Due to the drought, farming in America would cease.
    (2) Due to the drought, farming in America was prospering.
    (3) The Resettlement Administration helped union members.
    (4) Because of the Resettlement Administration, farmers would start factory jobs.
    (5) The Resettlement Administration offered farmers hope.

Question 6 refers to the following information.

Liberia is a West African state on the Atlantic coast of Africa, bordered by Sierra Leone, Guinea, and Ivory Coast. Liberia became the first black republic in Africa when it gained its independence in 1847. The state was an experiment supported by a private American organization, the U.S. government, and African leaders. The intent was to resettle freed American slaves in Africa, but the idea was not successful. By the 1980s, violent uprisings led to political, social, and economic chaos. Now, Liberia relies heavily on humanitarian aid from foreign governments.

6. What is the main topic of this passage?

    (1) the political structure of Liberia
    (2) the economy of Liberia
    (3) a brief history of Liberia
    (4) how Liberia was founded
    (5) famous Liberians

Question 7 refers to the following information.

During his presidency, Theodore Roosevelt worked to end monopolies, to settle labor-management disputes, and to strengthen government authority over several industries.

7. What does this information imply about Roosevelt's beliefs?

    (1) He thought that government should not interfere with business.
    (2) He supported government regulation.
    (3) He believed that corporations should make and follow their own rules.
    (4) He supported the growth of large powerful companies.
    (5) He opposed unions and strikes.

Sequence of Events

On the GED Social Studies Test, you will answer questions about sequence. **Sequence** is the order in which events occur. As you read the passage below, think about the sequence of events.

TIP

Questions about sequence often contain words like *when, next, after, before, first,* or *last.* To identify sequence in a passage, look for these words or dates or times.

Benjamin Franklin was born in Boston in 1706. As a boy, he was an apprentice to his brother, a newspaper publisher. At age 20, Franklin started his own newspaper. During his 20s and 30s, Franklin founded a library, a fire company, a college, an insurance company, and a hospital. At 45, he began nearly 40 years of service as a public official. When he was 48, Franklin performed his famous kite experiment that led to the discovery that lightning contained electricity. In his late 50s, Franklin reorganized the postal system of the American colonies. In 1776, Franklin helped draft the Declaration of Independence. For most of his 70s, he served as the first American minister to Paris. Finally, at age 81, he helped to write the Constitution of the United States. Franklin died in Philadelphia in 1790.

1. When did Benjamin Franklin start his own newspaper?

_____

2. According to the passage, what was Franklin's last accomplishment?

_____

1. Benjamin Franklin started his own newspaper at the age of 20.
2. Franklin's last accomplishment was helping to write the Constitution.

Remember that events are usually, but not always, told in the order in which they happened. To understand sequence, organize your ideas. If you are organizing a sequence of events over time, use a timeline like the one below. If you are organizing a sequence of steps in a process, use a sequence chart like the one on page 65.

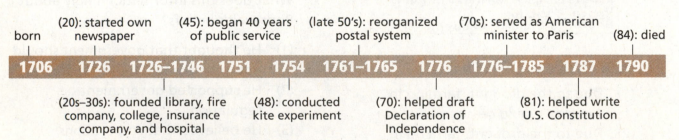

	(20): started own newspaper		(45): began 40 years of public service		(late 50's): reorganized postal system		(70s): served as American minister to Paris		
born									(84): died
1706	**1726**	**1726–1746**	**1751**	**1754**	**1761–1765**	**1776**	**1776–1785**	**1787**	**1790**
		(20s–30s): founded library, fire company, college, insurance company, and hospital		(48): conducted kite experiment		(70): helped draft Declaration of Independence		(81): helped write U.S. Constitution	

To identify sequence, ask yourself:
- In what order did things happen?
- What part of the sequence of events am I being asked to identify?

· ·

Have you ever followed directions to complete a process? What did you do first? What was the final step?

The cost of living is often determined by measuring the change in the prices of basic goods and services over time. The Consumer Price Index, or CPI, is a measurement used by the Bureau of Labor Statistics that shows the average change over time in the price of a specific group of goods. To determine the CPI, the Bureau first chooses a "market basket," or a representative sample of commonly purchased goods and services, such as food, housing, medical care, transportation, and entertainment. Then a reference year is established and the cost for that "market basket" is determined. Next, the cost of the same basket is determined for a later year. Finally, the Bureau compares these two costs to calculate the CPI for the later year and show the percentage change in the cost of the "market basket." The CPI is used to set wages, welfare benefits, and Social Security payments.

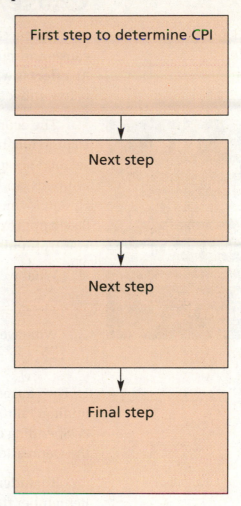

First step to determine CPI

Next step

Next step

Final step

GED PRACTICE   Choose the one best answer to the question.

To become a U.S. citizen, an immigrant must first have lived legally in the United States for three to five years. Then the immigrant can fill out an application for citizenship called a "petition for naturalization." Next, the applicant appears at a hearing before a government official to show that he or she believes in the principles of the U.S. Constitution. The applicant must also show a knowledge of English and familiarity with U.S. history and government. After their hearings, applicants can file their petitions for naturalization with the court.

Then they are called to court to take an oath of allegiance to the United States. This is the final step in the citizenship process.

1. What is the second step in the application process for becoming a U.S. citizen?

    (1) file a petition for naturalization
    (2) take an oath of allegiance
    (3) appear at a hearing
    (4) live three to five years in the United States
    (5) show a basic knowledge of U.S. history

Cause/Effect

On the GED Social Studies Test, you will answer questions about cause-and-effect relationships. A **cause** is what makes something happen. An **effect** is what happens as the result of a cause. As you read the passage below, think about the cause-and-effect relationships.

The economic depression of the 1930s, known as the Great Depression, had various causes. The years leading up to the Depression seemed prosperous, but problems existed. Agriculture, coal mining, railroads, and textiles were declining, and banks were failing. Unemployment rose as new technology eliminated jobs. The Depression lasted approximately ten years and finally ended when spending for World War II stimulated the economy.

1. What were the causes of the Great Depression?

2. What were the effects of spending during World War II?

1. The causes of the Great Depression were declines in agriculture, coal mining, railroads, and textiles; failing banks; and rising unemployment.
2. Spending during World War II stimulated the economy, which ended the Depression.

To understand cause and effect, organize your ideas in a chart. Remember that an effect can become the cause of another effect and that sometimes a cause can have more than one effect.

Cause ⟶	Effect
Business and industry declined; banks failed; new technology eliminated jobs	Great Depression began
Spending for World War II	Economy was stimulated
Economy was stimulated	Depression ended

To identify cause-and-effect relationships, ask yourself:
- What happened?
- What caused it to happen?

Think about a time that you caused something to happen. What did you do? What was the result?

Read the passage and add one cause and one effect to the chart. Then answer the questions.

   After World War II, Germany was divided. The western half became a democracy. East Germany remained under the control of the Soviet Union. Berlin, Germany's former capital, was located in East Germany. But it too was divided into a free western half and a communist East Berlin. Over the years thousands of East Germans escaped communism by fleeing to West Berlin. To stop this flight, in 1961 the Soviet Union built a concrete and barbed wire barrier around West Berlin. As the escapes continued, the wall became larger and more heavily guarded. The Berlin Wall stood for almost 30 years. In 1989 East Germany lifted restrictions on emigration. Germans celebrated by destroying the Berlin Wall.

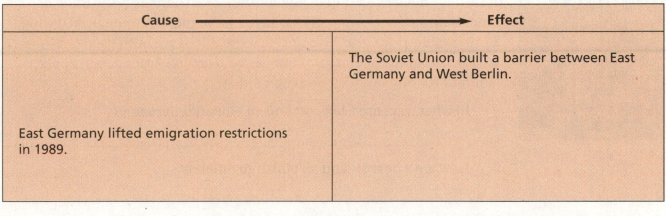

Cause ⟶	Effect
	The Soviet Union built a barrier between East Germany and West Berlin.
East Germany lifted emigration restrictions in 1989.	

1. Why did the Soviets build a barrier around West Berlin?

   _____

2. What happened when East Germany lifted emigration restrictions in 1989?

   _____

GED PRACTICE   Choose the **one best answer** to the question.

   The national debt is the money owed by the federal government to individuals, businesses, and other governments. This money is borrowed to cover budget deficits, or situations when spending exceeds income. Historically, deficits have been greatest during wars and recessions. Deficits are often the result of income-tax cuts combined with an increase in spending for military defense and public assistance programs. Between 1980 and 1990, the national debt more than tripled—rising from about $900 billion to over $3 trillion. In other words, the national debt in 1990 was $13,000 per person.

3. According to the passage, what is a common cause of budget deficits?

   (1) a combination of income-tax cuts and spending increases
   (2) an increase in the national debt
   (3) a combination of war and economic recession
   (4) borrowing money from other governments
   (5) a decrease in public-assistance programs

Compare/Contrast

On the GED Social Studies Test, you may be asked to compare and contrast. **Comparing** shows how things are the same, or similar. **Contrasting** shows how things are different. As you read the passage below, think about how things are similar and how they are different.

A boycott is used to pressure an individual, a group, or a nation into changing behavior. In an economic boycott, people refuse to buy certain products. A boycott can also be non-economic. For example, about 40 countries took part in a sports boycott of the 1980 Olympic Games to protest the Soviet invasion of Afghanistan. In an embargo, the trade of goods with another country is banned. Embargoes are often used during war to isolate a country. Boycotts and embargoes are both used to express disapproval or to encourage a change. Both acts are intended to apply economic or other pressure on their target.

1. In what ways are a boycott and an embargo the same?

_____

2. How are a boycott and an embargo different?

_____

1. They are both used to show disapproval, apply pressure, and cause change. 2. A boycott can be used against an individual, group, or country; an embargo is only used against a country. During a boycott, people refuse to buy a certain product or participate in an activity; in an embargo, the trade of goods is banned.

To compare and contrast two things, use a Venn diagram. Write things that are the same in the center. Write things that are different in each outside section.

Boycott   **Both**   **Embargo**

Used against individual, group, or country
Refusal to buy or participate
Can be non-economic

Used to show disapproval, apply pressure, and cause change

Used only against a foreign country
Prohibits selling
Only economic

To compare and contrast, ask yourself:
*   What two things am I comparing and contrasting?
*   How are they similar? How are they different?

. . . .

Think about two people you know. In what ways are those two people similar? In what ways are they different?

SKILL PRACTICE   Read the passage, complete the Venn diagram, and answer the questions.

The Nile River and the Panama Canal are both important waterways. While the Nile River is naturally occurring, the Panama Canal is a man-made passage. Each waterway contributes greatly to its country's economy. Most of Egypt's population lives within the Nile's basin, using its water for farming, fishing, and raising cattle and camels. However, only about 50 percent of the Nile River can be navigated. The Panama Canal serves as a passage between the Atlantic and Pacific Oceans. It was built so that ships can travel its entire length. For 85 years, Panama received millions of dollars in "rent" paid by the United States for the use of the canal.

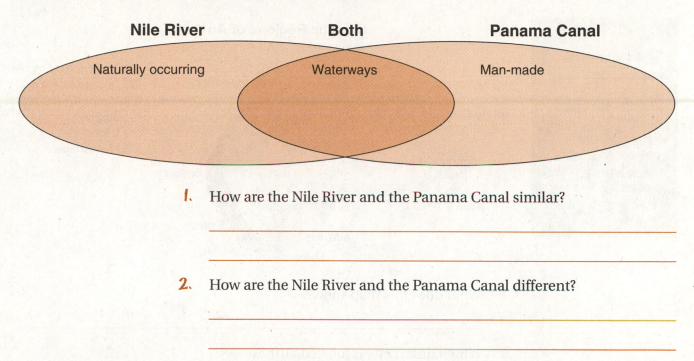

Nile River   **Both**   **Panama Canal**

Naturally occurring   Waterways   Man-made

1. How are the Nile River and the Panama Canal similar?

_____

_____

2. How are the Nile River and the Panama Canal different?

_____

_____

GED PRACTICE   Choose the one best answer to the question.

The Napoleonic Code was adopted as a national legal code for France in 1804. The code was divided into three parts. The first section dealt with personal rights, property, and education. The second section covered the right of the government to take private property for public use, and it abolished feudalism and class privileges. The final section of the Napoleonic Code covered inheritance, gifts, and contracts. In later years more codes were added. This code has served as a model for many governments in Europe and Latin America.

3. How are the first and second sections of the Napoleonic Code similar?

(1) They were both written after 1804.
(2) They were both based on the U.S. Constitution.
(3) They both contained laws about inheritance.
(4) They both dealt with property rights.
(5) They were both later abolished.

COMPARE/CONTRAST

Check your answers on page 159.

Lesson 20

Maps

Maps usually show geographical regions. However, maps can also show political boundaries, historical changes in population or ideas, information about climate, routes traveled by people, or the distribution of resources. The GED Social Studies Test includes questions about interpreting these kinds of maps. Look at the map below and answer the questions.

TIP

Look carefully at the title and the key of a map. The title will tell you what the map is about, and the key will help you read and understand the information on the map.

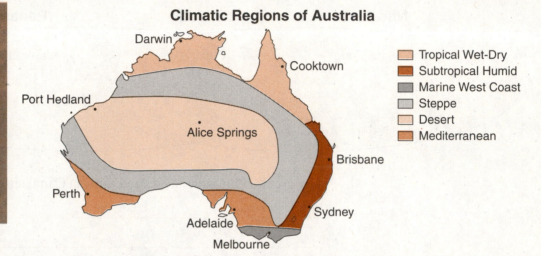

Climatic Regions of Australia

Key:
- Tropical Wet-Dry
- Subtropical Humid
- Marine West Coast
- Steppe
- Desert
- Mediterranean

1. What does this map show?

_____

2. Which desert city is located farthest west?

_____

3. Which city has the same climate as Perth?

_____

1. The map shows the climatic regions of Australia. 2. The desert city that is located farthest west is Port Hedland. 3. Adelaide has the same climate as Perth.

When you read a map, ask yourself:
- What information is shown on this map?
- What knowledge can I gain from this map?

Have you ever used a map to plan a trip? Where did you go? How did the map help you?

Read the information, look at the map, and answer the questions.

Sir Ernest Shackleton was an explorer who made two unsuccessful attempts to reach the South Pole.

Antarctic Expeditions of Sir Ernest Shackleton

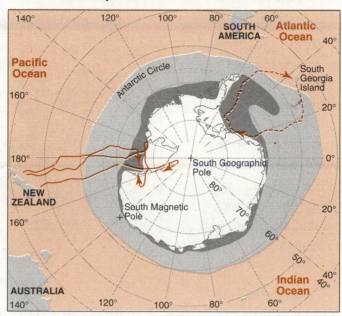
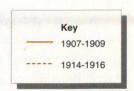

1. What does this map show? _____

2. On which expedition did Shackleton come closer to the South Geographic Pole? _____

3. Where did Shackleton begin and end his second expedition?

   _____

GED PRACTICE **Choose the one best answer to the question.**

Countries of Scandinavia

4. According to this map, which Scandinavian capital city is located farthest south?

   (1) Copenhagen
   (2) Oslo
   (3) Stockholm
   (4) Odense
   (5) Bergen

Social Studies Skills Practice 2

Directions: Choose the <u>one best</u> answer to each question.

Questions 1 and 2 refer to the following information.

Marco Polo was an Italian explorer who brought a wide variety of useful inventions to Europe from the Far East. As a teenager, Marco Polo accompanied his father and his uncle on a trip to Asia. After befriending the emperor of China, Marco Polo traveled around China for 17 years as an aide to the emperor. Finally, Marco Polo returned to Venice. He brought with him many Chinese innovations like fireworks, paper currency, the idea of using coal for heat and fuel, and noodles. The Italians embraced these items enthusiastically.

1. What happened after Marco Polo befriended the emperor of China?

   (1) He went on a trip with his father and his uncle.
   (2) He invented fireworks and noodles.
   (3) He discouraged Italians from using coal for heat and fuel.
   (4) He decided to learn as many foreign languages as possible.
   (5) He traveled around China as the emperor's aide.

2. According to the passage, what was an effect of Marco Polo's travels?

   (1) His father began to travel.
   (2) The Italians gained access to many Chinese innovations.
   (3) The Italians and the Chinese formed a military alliance.
   (4) Italians began to immigrate to China.
   (5) The Chinese learned about Italian inventions.

Questions 3 and 4 refer to the following map.

Average Daily Temperatures (January)

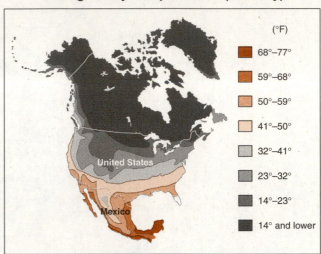

3. How do the daily temperatures in Canada compare to those in Mexico?

   (1) They are approximately the same.
   (2) Canada's are slightly lower.
   (3) Canada's are much lower.
   (4) Canada's are slightly higher.
   (5) Canada's are much higher.

4. What is one difference between the temperatures in Canada and the temperatures in the United States?

   (1) The temperatures in the U.S. tend to be much lower than the temperatures in Canada.
   (2) The coldest regions of the U.S. cover more area than the coldest regions of Canada.
   (3) Only Canada has areas that reach temperatures below 14°F.
   (4) There is a much greater range of temperatures in the U.S.
   (5) All of Canada's temperatures are below freezing, but all U.S. temperatures are above freezing.

Questions 5 and 6 refer to the following map.

Languages of South America

5. Based on the map, what is one result of the European colonization of South America?

    (1) All South Americans speak Spanish or Portuguese.
    (2) American Indians colonized South America after the Europeans.
    (3) There are no remaining aboriginal (native) South American languages.
    (4) Spain made political allies of the South American nations.
    (5) European languages are spoken in much of South America.

6. What type of map would best compare the languages of South America with their country of origin?

    (1) a world map showing all countries
    (2) a map showing the climates of South America
    (3) a map showing the European settlement of South America
    (4) a map of Europe showing all countries
    (5) a current map of South America listing countries and cities

Questions 7 and 8 refer to the following information.

The first ten amendments to the Constitution, the Bill of Rights, provide legal protection for basic individual rights. The Constitution did not originally protect individual rights, and many people openly expressed their displeasure. So after the Constitution was ratified, several states proposed amendments to protect individual rights. As a result, the Congress proposed a Bill of Rights to include these amendments. James Madison, who drafted the amendments, said that they would provide "securities for liberty" and would "declare the great rights of mankind." Madison intended for revisions to be made to the body of the Constitution. Instead the new amendments were added at the end of the document.

7. Which of the following happened last?

    (1) The Constitution was written.
    (2) The Constitution was rewritten to include protection for basic individual rights.
    (3) Several states wanted amendments to the Constitution.
    (4) The Bill of Rights was adopted.
    (5) Congress drafted the Bill of Rights.

8. Why did Congress add the Bill of Rights to the Constitution?

    (1) James Madison refused to support the Constitution until changes were made.
    (2) In a public election, Americans voted in favor of the change.
    (3) Many Americans wanted the Constitution to provide protection for basic individual rights.
    (4) The Bill of Rights clarified provisions of the original Constitution.
    (5) The Bill of Rights explained punishments for breaking the laws of the Constitution.

Adequacy of Data

On the GED Social Studies Test, you will answer questions that ask you to evaluate the **adequacy of data.** You will be asked if there is enough information to support a conclusion. Read the passage below. Then think about the adequacy of the data.

The Statue of Liberty is a well-known symbol of America. Gustave Eiffel, who also designed the Eiffel Tower in Paris, designed the interior scaffolding of the Statue of Liberty. French sculptor Frederic Auguste Bartholdi designed the outer shell. Richard Morris Hunt, an American, designed the pedestal. The statue was a gift from France in honor of America's 1876 centennial. French citizens donated money to build the statue, and Americans donated funds for the pedestal. The statue was shipped from France in pieces, then assembled on an island in New York Harbor.

TIP
To answer test questions, first rule out any choices that are clearly not supported by the given information. Then decide which of the remaining choices is best supported by the given information.

1. Does the passage support the conclusion that the statue cost more than the base?

2. What evidence supports the conclusion that France and the United States were friends in 1876?

1. No. The passage tells how each piece was paid for, but not how much each piece cost. 2. The conclusion that France and the U.S. were friends in 1876 is supported by the statement that the statue was a gift from France.

To understand adequacy of data, use a chart. List the important details from the selection and any important relationships between them. Think about conclusions that can be supported or verified by the details.

Important Details
• Scaffolding by Eiffel (Fr.); shell by Bartholdi (Fr.); pedestal by Hunt (U.S.)
• Gift from France for 1876 centennial
• French citizens paid for statue; Americans paid for pedestal
• Shipped in pieces; assembled on island in New York Harbor

To evaluate the adequacy of data, ask yourself:
- What details are given? What are the relationships between these details?
- Do I have enough information to support or verify a conclusion?

Think about a recent decision you made. Did you have enough information to make it? What additional information would have been helpful?

The first national minimum wage act was the Fair Labor Standards Act of 1938. This set the minimum wage at $0.25 per hour. The act was originally intended to stop wage cutting during the Depression. Over the years, Congress has raised the minimum wage a number of times. Some opponents of minimum wage laws claim that a minimum wage leads to rising inflation and a decrease in entry-level jobs. The national minimum wage was first raised in 1950 to $0.75 per hour. There were 17 additional raises between 1955 and 1997, when it was raised to $5.15 per hour.

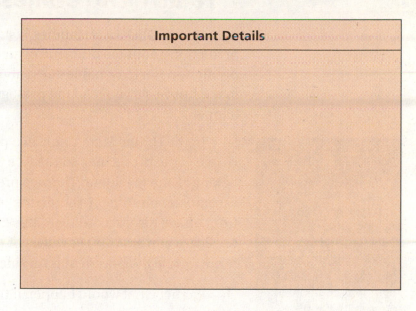

Important Details

I. What evidence from the passage supports the conclusion that not everyone agrees with minimum wage laws?

_____

2. What additional evidence is needed to verify the conclusion that unemployment rates are directly related to minimum wage rates?

_____

_____

GED PRACTICE   Choose the <u>one best answer</u> to the question.

The Tennessee Valley Authority, or TVA, was created in 1933 to oversee hydroelectric facilities in north Alabama and to provide navigation and flood control for the Tennessee River. Over seven decades, the TVA has also improved farm and forestry practices, produced and distributed fertilizer, and established numerous recreational facilities. TVA dams indirectly help control flooding on the Ohio and Mississippi Rivers and produce hydroelectric power for over three million people.

3. Is there enough evidence to support the conclusion that the TVA is the sole source of electricity in the Tennessee Valley?

(1) No, the total number of electricity users is needed.

(2) Yes, the TVA provides hydroelectric power for 3 million customers.

(3) Yes, the TVA runs hydroelectric facilities.

(4) No, a map of Tennessee is needed.

(5) No, the TVA has too many other responsibilities to be the sole supplier.

Predict Outcomes

On the GED Social Studies Test, you may be asked to make a prediction about the outcome of an event or a sequence of events. A **prediction** is a reasonable guess about what will happen next or sometime in the future. As you read the passage below, think about what is likely to happen.

In the United States, only two positions are elected by all voters in the country: the president and the vice president. Most executive duties belong to the president. The vice president's main role is to be ready to assume the presidency should the president die, resign, or be removed from office. Also, according to the 25th Amendment (1967) the vice president can assume the duties of the president—not the presidency itself—while the president is disabled.

TIP

When predicting outcomes, remember that you do not have to know exactly what *will* happen. You just need to make a guess about what is *likely* to happen.

1. Predict what would happen if the president were removed from office.

   _____

2. Predict what might happen if the president had to be unconscious for 12 hours for a medical procedure.

   _____

1. If the president were removed from office, the vice president would become president. 2. If the president had to be unconscious for 12 hours for a medical procedure, the vice president might temporarily assume the duties of the president.

To predict outcomes, use a chart. List the events that have already happened in the first column and your predictions in the second column.

Event ⟶	ediction
• President is removed from office • President is disabled for medical procedure	• Vice president assumes presidency • Vice president assumes presidential duties temporarily

To predict outcomes, ask yourself:
- What has already happened?
- What is likely to happen next?

Have you ever predicted the outcome of a book or movie? What did you predict? What led to this prediction?

SKILL PRACTICE   Read the passage, complete the chart, and answer the questions.

The tusks of elephants, walruses, whales, and boars are made of ivory. Because it is easy to carve and shines nicely when polished, ivory has been popular for thousands of years. It has been used to make jewelry, buttons, billiard balls, piano keys, and other items. The most favored type of ivory is that of East African elephants. To stop the killing of elephants, over 100 nations banned the trade of elephant ivory in 1989. However, the illegal ivory trade continues. In an effort to reduce poaching, or the illegal killing of game animals, substitutes have been developed. Vegetable ivory is made from the South American ivory nut palm. Celluloid and plastic substitutes have been created as well.

Event ⟶	Prediction
• Illegal ivory trade increases	•
• Artificial ivory developed	•

1. Predict the most likely result of increases in the illegal ivory trade.

   _____

2. What might happen if scientists developed an artificial ivory with properties that were identical to those of real tusk ivory?

   _____

GED PRACTICE   Choose the one best answer to the question.

Each morning, children in the United States recite the Pledge of Allegiance. Originally published in a magazine in 1892, the identity of the author was unknown until 1939. That is when Francis Bellamy, a former employee of the magazine, was credited with writing the pledge. The original text has been altered twice. In 1923, the phrase "my flag" was changed to "the flag of the United States of America." In 1954, an act of Congress added the words "under God." At the beginning of the 21st century, a movement was begun to remove "under God" from the pledge. As of the writing of this text, the phrase remains.

3. In a 2002 survey, 79 percent of Americans surveyed were in favor of keeping the words "under God" in the Pledge of Allegiance.

   What would be the most likely outcome of a national vote on this matter?

   The vote would

   (1) declare the 1954 act to be unconstitutional
   (2) select a new Pledge of Allegiance
   (3) remove the words when the pledge is recited in public schools
   (4) keep the 1954 version of the pledge
   (5) restore the pledge to its original version

PREDICT OUTCOMES

Application

On the GED Social Studies Test, you will answer questions that ask you to apply information to a new situation. Use ideas that are presented in one situation to understand a different but similar situation. Read the passage below.

The period between 1920 and 1933 is known as the Prohibition era. In 1919, the adoption of the 18th Amendment made the manufacture, sale, and transportation of alcoholic beverages illegal. Prohibition, which was a response to the public opinion that alcohol destroyed lives and disrupted families, was a great failure. Bootleggers illegally produced and distributed alcohol. Speakeasies, illegal establishments where people could buy and drink alcohol, sprung up everywhere. Most of this illegal commerce was run by organized crime. When it became clear that the experiment had only succeeded in causing a rise in criminal activity, Prohibition ended in 1933 through the adoption of the 21st Amendment. This is the only amendment that was adopted in order to repeal an earlier one.

1. What happens when a government tries to legislate behavior?

_____

2. If an amendment outlawing smoking existed, what might happen?

_____

1. When a government tries to legislate people's behavior, people do not always change their behavior. 2. If an amendment outlawing smoking existed, people would probably continue to smoke illegally.

To apply information to a new situation, use a chart. Write the idea from the given information in one column and the application to a new situation in another column.

Idea from Given Information	Application to New Situation
When a government tries to legislate behavior, people do not always change their behavior.	If an amendment outlawing smoking existed, people would continue to smoke illegally.

To apply information to a new situation, ask yourself:
- What do I know from one situation?
- How can I use this information in a new situation?

Have you ever learned something by making a mistake? How did the mistake help you deal with a similar situation later?

The Geneva Conventions are international agreements that apply during times of war. The conventions provide for the humane treatment of the wounded, prisoners of war, and civilians. Sixteen countries signed the first convention in Geneva in 1864. The signers promised to respect civilians and medical personnel, and to treat the wounded humanely. Conventions have been added since then to cover subjects like maritime war and prisoners of war. A convention added in 1949 allowed for the establishment of a war crimes tribunal. This set up a process for judging those accused of war crimes against civilians.

Idea from Given Information	Application to New Situation
The 1949 convention allowed for the establishment of a war crimes tribunal.	
Additional conventions have been added to establish international rules for actions during wartime.	

1. Based on the passage, what might be the consequences for former Yugoslavian leaders who may have committed war crimes in Bosnia in the 1990s?

   _____

2. What could be done to establish international rules for the distribution of humanitarian aid during times of war?

   _____

GED PRACTICE   Choose the <u>one best answer</u> to the question.

The Great Wall of China is the largest man-made structure in the world. Large enough to be seen from spacecraft in orbit, the wall spans 1,500 miles. The wall was originally the idea of an emperor who had it built in the third century B.C. by linking smaller existing walls. His intent was to mark the border of Chinese territory and to prevent invasion. Along the wall are gates, which were once popular trading posts. Later rulers expanded the wall over the centuries.

3. The first European city in North America, St. Augustine, was surrounded by a wall.

   Based on the passage, what is the most likely reason the wall was built?

   (1) to keep slaves from escaping
   (2) to protect the city from floods
   (3) to protect the city from attack
   (4) to create a close-knit community
   (5) to control trade

Bar Graphs and Line Graphs

A graph is a diagram used to display numerical data. A **bar graph** usually compares information. A **line graph** usually shows changes in information over time. The GED Social Studies Test includes both kinds of graphs. Read the information and look at the graph below. Then answer the questions.

TIP

When you look at bar or line graphs, be sure to read the labels on each axis. The labels will help you understand what the data is showing.

By the 1990s, about 800,000 miles of railway were in use in the world.

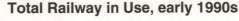

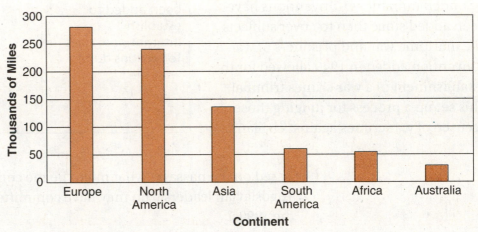

Total Railway in Use, early 1990s

1. What does this graph show?

   _____

2. About how many miles of railway were in use in Africa in the early 1990s?

   _____

1. The graph shows the miles of railway in use in the early 1990s, compared by continent. 2. About 50,000 miles of railway were in use in Africa in the early 1990s.

When you read a bar graph or line graph, ask yourself:

- What kind of graph is this? What kind of information does it show?

- What does the information in this graph tell me?

Have you ever seen a bar or line graph in a newspaper? What did you learn from it?

Read the information and look at the graph. Then answer the questions.

At one time, gold was used as a direct guarantee for paper currency. Gold is no longer the basis for currency in most nations, but many still hold gold in reserve.

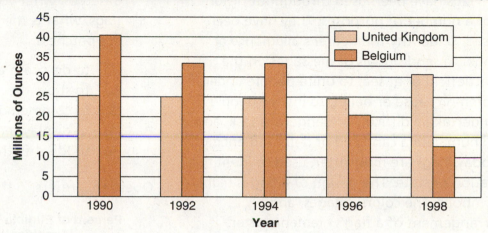

Reserves of Gold Held by the United Kingdom and Belgium (1990s)

1. What does this graph show?

_____

2. In what year did Belgium have the highest amount of gold in reserve?

_____

3. Based on the information in the graph, how would you summarize the United Kingdom's gold reserves for most of the 1990s?

_____

GED PRACTICE Choose the one best answer to the question.

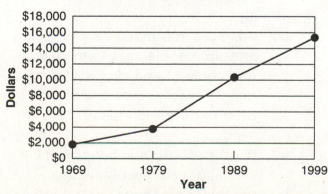

Average Yearly Tuition for Private Colleges (U.S.)

4. Based on the line graph, which of the following is the most reasonable prediction about tuition at a private college in 2009?

   (1) Not enough information is given to make a prediction.
   (2) The cost will be greater than $16,000.
   (3) The cost will be less than $15,000.
   (4) The cost will be about $60,000.
   (5) The cost will remain at about $15,000.

GRAPHIC SKILL: BAR GRAPHS AND LINE GRAPHS   Check your answers on page 161.   **81**

Social Studies Skills Practice 3

Directions: Choose the <u>one best</u> answer to each question.

Questions 1 and 2 refer to the following information.

Flags have been used throughout history for a number of purposes. They have been used to identify the bearer's allegiance or rank, to send signals or messages on the battlefield or at sea, to unite people under a common cause or belief, to inspire people to undertake a difficult or dangerous task, and to humiliate a captured or defeated enemy. Today, flags are most often used to identify a nation or state. The design of a flag is highly symbolic. The colors, images, and arrangement of a flag's elements often express the ideals, beliefs, and history of its bearer. Though some flags are incredibly complex and highly embellished, most flags are simple so that they are easily identified, especially at sea or from a great distance. The earliest flags consisted of a pole with a carved emblem or symbol at the top and ribbons attached below the carving.

1. Suppose the United States established a colony on the moon. Based on the passage, what is the most likely description of the colony's flag?

   (1) a flag with a dark background, to signify space, and an American flag in the corner, to symbolize the history of the colonists
   (2) a pole with a carved lion at the top and green ribbons attached to the bottom
   (3) a flag with a highly-detailed image of the moon in the center and a red background, to signify bravery
   (4) a white flag to represent the surrender of the new colonists
   (5) a flag with a four-colored rectangle to represent all of humanity

2. Military units often have distinct patches that soldiers wear on their uniforms. Based on what you have learned about flags, what is the most likely purpose of the patches?

   (1) to decorate the soldiers' uniforms
   (2) to show the soldiers' patriotism
   (3) to commemorate a leader
   (4) to display secret messages
   (5) to identify the soldiers' unit

Question 3 refers to the following graph.

Percent of Eligible Voters Who Voted in Presidential Elections

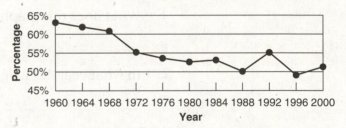

3. In 1971, the 26th Amendment to the U.S. Constitution lowered the voting age from 21 to 18. Does the graph support the idea that people younger than 21 vote less often than people 21 and over?

   (1) Yes, the graph provides the necessary evidence to support the idea.
   (2) No, more information about voting rates for people ages 18 to 20 and for people 21 and over is needed.
   (3) No, the exact percentage of total voter participation for 1972 is needed.
   (4) No, the specific number of eligible voters for each year is needed.
   (5) No, the graph shows that young people are the most frequent voters.

Questions 4 and 5 refer to the following graphs.

Expeditions to Polar Regions

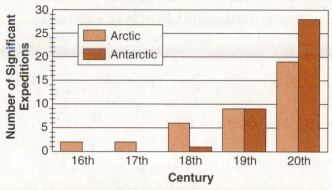

4. What information could be used to support the idea that improved technology helped increase polar exploration?

    (1) data about the explorers in each century
    (2) data about the dates and lengths of expeditions to each region
    (3) data about explorers' home countries
    (4) data about the kind of equipment used in polar exploration with dates of invention
    (5) data about the costs of polar expeditions

5. Based on data in the graph, what is the most reasonable prediction about the number of polar expeditions in the 21st century?

    (1) Arctic expeditions will increase; Antarctic expeditions will decrease.
    (2) Arctic expeditions will decrease; Antarctic expeditions will increase.
    (3) Antarctic and Arctic expeditions will both increase only slightly.
    (4) Arctic and Antarctic expeditions will both decrease.
    (5) Antarctic expeditions will increase more than Arctic ones.

Questions 6 and 7 refer to the following information.

Credit cards, introduced in the 1950s, became especially popular at the end of the century. Between 1980 and 2000, credit card debt in the United States rose from about $55 billion to more than $660 billion. Some people also use "debit" cards. These are printed with the logos of major credit cards and are processed through the same systems. However, instead of offering credit that must be repaid, debit cards use funds from a cardholder's bank account. Accordingly, the consumer isn't charged interest, since money is not being borrowed.

6. Does this passage provide enough evidence to draw a conclusion about whether consumers prefer debit cards or credit cards?

    (1) Yes, the passage states that debit cards cost more than credit cards.
    (2) No, information about the number of people who use each card is needed.
    (3) Yes, the rising amount of credit card debt implies a preference for credit cards.
    (4) Yes, since debit cards don't charge interest, they are more popular.
    (5) No, the passage needs to include the date that debit cards were introduced.

7. An unsecured loan is one for which no collateral, or security for the loan, is offered. A credit card account is an example of an unsecured loan. Which of the following is also an example of an unsecured loan?

    (1) a new car loan
    (2) a mortgage loan to buy a home
    (3) a student loan for college
    (4) a mobile home loan
    (5) a used-car loan

Fact and Opinion

On the GED Social Studies Test, you will answer questions that ask you to distinguish fact from opinion. A **fact** is an idea that can be proven to be true. An **opinion** is what someone thinks, feels, or believes. You can agree or disagree with an opinion, but a fact cannot be argued. Read the following passage. Then answer the questions.

On September 16, 1620, a group of courageous voyagers began their journey to America. About 100 passengers set out aboard the Mayflower, facing a dangerous 65-day ocean crossing. The Pilgrims had been granted land in America, but when they landed in November, they could not reach it. They wisely decided to stay where they had landed. The settlers wrote and signed the Mayflower Compact, which established a government for their small settlement. That was the beginning of what would become the greatest democracy in the world.

1. What opinion does the first sentence give about the Pilgrims?

_____

2. What fact in the second sentence supports this opinion?

_____

1. The first sentence calls the Pilgrims courageous voyagers. 2. The second sentence describes their journey as 65 days long.

To understand fact and opinion, make a chart. Write facts from the passage in the first column and opinions in the second column.

Facts	Opinions
• Voyage began Sept.16,1620 • 100 passengers on Mayflower • 65-day ocean crossing • Pilgrims granted land in America • Decided to stay where they landed • Wrote and signed Mayflower Compact	• Voyagers were courageous • Ocean crossing was dangerous • Settlers' decision was wise • Greatest democracy began

To identify facts and opinions, ask yourself:
- Can this information be proven to be true?
- Is this what someone thinks, feels, or believes?

Think about a time when you gave your opinion. What facts helped you form that opinion?

Read the passage and complete the chart.

In 1791, George Washington selected the site for a permanent capital of the United States. By selecting a site very close to the geographic center of the thirteen original colonies, Washington demonstrated political brilliance. Washington, D.C., is unique because it was entirely planned from the beginning. When the area was chosen, French engineer Pierre Charles L'Enfant was hired to plan the city. He designed a plan for streets, the sites for government buildings, and a number of squares and circles for monuments and memorials. With its parks, museums, lakes, and cherry trees, Washington, D.C., remains one of the most important and beautiful cities in the United States.

Facts	Opinions

GED PRACTICE Choose the one best answer to the question.

Robert Edward "Ted" Turner is one of America's most successful businesspeople. His innovative idea of offering 24-hour news coverage through his cable television station CNN is just one reason people consider him a business genius. Turner is also an avid sportsman. He has participated in the America's Cup yacht race, and he owns the Atlanta Braves. In addition to his invaluable contributions to media and sports, Turner is a humanitarian. In 1986, he sponsored the Goodwill Games in Moscow to promote international peace.

1. Which of the following is an opinion?

   (1) Ted Turner is one of America's most successful businesspeople.
   (2) The cable television station CNN offers 24-hour news coverage.
   (3) Ted Turner participates in sports.
   (4) Ted Turner owns the Atlanta Braves.
   (5) Ted Turner sponsored the Goodwill Games to promote international peace.

Values and Beliefs

On the GED Social Studies Test, you will be asked about values and beliefs. **Values and beliefs** are ideas that a person holds true and uses to make decisions or form opinions. As you read the passage below, think about values and beliefs.

English philosopher John Locke introduced the idea of people's fundamental rights in the 17th century. Locke believed individuals had certain rights, such as the rights of life, freedom, and property, that government should protect. In America, Thomas Jefferson expanded on Locke's views by emphasizing the importance of human happiness and religious freedom. Jefferson incorporated Locke's ideas into the Declaration of Independence in 1776. In 1789, French revolutionaries who were inspired by Locke's ideas issued the Declaration of the Rights of Man, which stated that "men are born and remain free and equal in rights." It also stated that it was the responsibility of the government to assure these rights, including "liberty, property, security, and resistance to oppression."

1. How did Thomas Jefferson expand on Locke's views?

_____

2. What does the French declaration show that the people of France valued?

_____

1. Jefferson expanded on Locke's views by emphasizing the rights of happiness and religious freedom. 2. The declaration shows that the French valued people's fundamental rights.

To understand values and beliefs, organize your ideas in a chart. List the values and beliefs of the people you read about.

Subject	Values and Beliefs
John Locke	Individuals have certain rights that should be protected by government
Thomas Jefferson	Rights also include human happiness and religious freedom
French revolutionaries	"Men are born and remain free and equal in rights" Government assures and protects rights of liberty, property, security, and resistance to oppression

To identify values and beliefs, ask yourself:

• What does this person believe? What does this person value?

• What is the relationship between a person's values and decisions?

Have you ever made a decision based on a value or belief? What was the decision? On what value or belief was it based?

Read the passage, complete the chart, and answer the questions.

The Great Seal is the official seal of the United States. In 1776, the Continental Congress appointed a committee to design such a seal. Congress didn't approve any of the committee's ideas, so a second committee was appointed. None of its designs were accepted, either. Finally, a third committee, appointed in 1782, designed the seal that is still in use today. The front shows an eagle with a shield of 13 red and white stripes. The eagle holds an olive branch in its right talon to signify peace and a bundle of 13 arrows in its left talon to signify might. The seal's reverse side shows an unfinished 13-step pyramid with an eye above it. Both sides of the seal appear on the back of a one-dollar bill. Other than the dollar bill, the Great Seal is only affixed to treaties, official diplomatic documents, and letters from the president to foreign leaders.

Subject	Values and Beliefs
Continental Congress and Great Seal designers	
Today's government	

1. Based on the information in the passage, what beliefs and values were important to the people who designed and approved the Great Seal?

   _____

2. What do the uses of the seal show about how it is valued by the government?

   _____

Choose the one best answer to the question.

A monopoly is the exclusive control of a product or service by a single seller. In the United States most monopolies are illegal. A free market depends on sellers competing to offer fair and comparable prices. If just one seller controls a single product or service, there is no competition. The seller could control the selling price and set the price as high as he or she wanted to. Consumers would have to pay that high price because they could not obtain the product or service elsewhere for a lower price.

3. Based on the information in the passage, which of the following statements is true?

   (1) The U.S. government values low prices.
   (2) Consumers do not value choice.
   (3) Sellers value competition.
   (4) Sellers value the opportunity to form monopolies.
   (5) The U.S. government values a free market.

Political Cartoons

Political cartoons are drawings that express artists' opinions about the world, especially politics and current events. The GED Social Studies Test includes political cartoons. Look at the political cartoon below and answer the questions.

1. In this cartoon, what do the donkey and the elephant represent?

   _____

   _____

2. What is Morin's opinion about campaign finance reform?

   _____

   _____

1. The donkey represents the Democratic party, and the elephant represents the Republican party. 2. Morin thinks that politicians who hold corporations responsible for financial misdeeds should also work to be more responsible themselves by reforming the financing of political campaigns.

When you interpret a political cartoon, ask yourself:

● What is happening in the cartoon?

● What is the artist's message?

Think about a political cartoon you have seen recently. What was it about? What was the artist's opinion?

1. What is the topic of this cartoon?

   _____

2. What does the tree in the right half of the cartoon represent?

   _____

3. What relationship does the cartoonist suggest between the two parts of the cartoon?

   _____

   _____

GED PRACTICE   Choose the <u>one best answer</u> to the question.

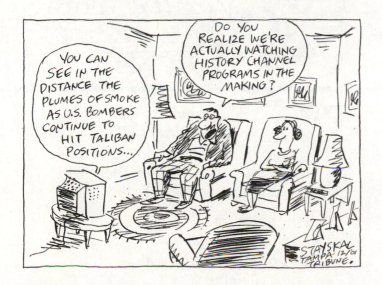

4. What point is the artist who drew this cartoon trying to make?

   (1) The media has a significant effect on the outcome of international conflict.

   (2) The United States should not become involved in other countries' problems.

   (3) Because of media coverage, Americans today can view wars as they happen, rather than as programs at a later date.

   (4) Americans watch too much television.

   (5) The same technologies that provide cable television help the military succeed in battle.

Social Studies Skills Practice 4

Directions: Choose the one best answer to each question.

<u>Questions 1 through 3</u> refer to the following information.

Historians believe that the Chinese invented both coins and paper currency. Coins have been used for almost 3,000 years, but paper currency has only been in existence for about 1,000 years. The Romans and many other ancient cultures had highly developed and organized banking and credit systems. Less successful cultures only recently began using coins and paper currency. In Africa, for example, cowry shells were used as currency long after other cultures began using the more convenient system of coins and paper currency.

1. Which of the following is an opinion?

    (1) Coins have been used for almost 3,000 years.
    (2) Paper currency has been used for about 1,000 years.
    (3) Less successful cultures only recently began using coins and paper currency.
    (4) Ancient cultures had organized banking and credit systems.
    (5) Cowry shells were used in Africa after coins and paper currency were invented.

2. Which of the following is a fact?

    (1) Coins are more convenient than shells.
    (2) Paper currency is the most convenient.
    (3) Roman banks were highly developed.
    (4) Cowry shells were less reliable as currency.
    (5) Both coins and paper currency have been used for 1,000 years or more.

3. Based on the passage, which of the following is true?

    (1) Many ancient cultures valued an organized system of currency.
    (2) Many ancient cultures valued paper.
    (3) Many African cultures valued an organized system of currency.
    (4) Many African cultures valued coins.
    (5) Many ancient cultures valued cowry shells.

<u>Question 4</u> refers to the following political cartoon.

In the cartoon below, the tank is labeled "MILITARY TRIBUNALS." Military tribunals are military courts that operate under different rules than civilian courts.

4. In the cartoon, what does the U.S. Constitution symbolize?

    (1) terrorism
    (2) international law
    (3) government officials
    (4) civil rights
    (5) American military power

Questions 5 and 6 refer to the following political cartoon.

This cartoon appeared in the *San Diego Union-Tribune* shortly after the terrorist attacks of September 11, 2001.

5. What does the eagle represent?

(1) the people of the world, united in their outrage
(2) the airline industry, suffering from financial setbacks
(3) the U.S. government, passing new laws
(4) the American people, grieving
(5) the American nation, preparing for war

6. What does this cartoon show that the artist believes?

(1) The American people are strong and determined.
(2) Watching and waiting is most important.
(3) The American economy is vulnerable to attack.
(4) The U.S. government needs to think carefully about future actions.
(5) The judicial system isn't doing enough to combat terrorism.

Questions 7 and 8 refer to the following information.

The town meeting is perhaps the purest form of democracy. First instituted in Massachusetts, this form of town government allows each citizen to speak, debate, and vote on legislation. In colonial times, town meetings were usually held weekly. Today, town meetings are generally held once each year. Between meetings, elected officials, called selectmen, carry out the decisions of the townspeople. Generally, all qualified town voters can attend and participate in a town meeting. For this reason, town meetings cannot work in large cities. Attempting to allow every voter in a large city a chance to speak, debate, and vote on issues would certainly be inefficient and chaotic.

7. Which of the following is an opinion?

(1) Town meetings were first instituted in Massachusetts.
(2) Colonial town meetings were usually held weekly.
(3) Selectmen carry out the decisions of the townspeople.
(4) Town meetings in a large city would certainly be inefficient and chaotic.
(5) Town meetings are still held in New England.

8. What fact supports the opinion that the town meeting is the purest form of democracy?

(1) Town meetings have been held since colonial times.
(2) Town meetings would not work in large cities.
(3) Town meetings allow each citizen to speak, debate, and vote on legislation.
(4) Selectmen carry out the townspeople's decisions between meetings.
(5) Town meetings are held once a year.

Mini-Test • Unit 2

This is a fifteen-minute practice test. After fifteen minutes, mark the last number you finished. Then complete the test and check your answers. If most of your answers were correct but you did not finish, try to work faster next time.

Directions: Choose the one best answer to each question.

Questions 1 and 2 refer to the following bar graph.

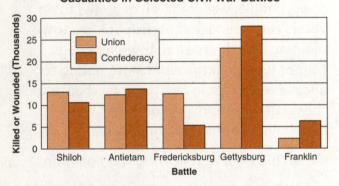

Casualties in Selected Civil War Battles

1. Which two battles show the most dramatic difference in Union casualties?

    (1) Fredericksburg and Gettysburg
    (2) Fredericksburg and Antietam
    (3) Shiloh and Franklin
    (4) Franklin and Gettysburg
    (5) Gettysburg and Shiloh

2. If you wanted to show Confederate casualties, from highest to lowest, which would be the first two battles on the list?

    (1) Fredericksburg, Franklin
    (2) Gettysburg, Antietam
    (3) Shiloh, Antietam
    (4) Shiloh, Gettysburg
    (5) Franklin, Fredericksburg

Questions 3 and 4 refer to the following information.

Division of labor is key idea in modern economics. More than 200 years ago, Adam Smith wrote about the idea, citing a pin-making factory as an example. He showed that the business could produce far more pins if each step were handled by a different worker—a worker who did that one task—than if one worker made each pin in its entirety. Smith believed that division of labor was the most important factor in improving a nation's standard of living.

3. Which of the following statements is a fact?

    (1) A business that does not use division of labor is sure to fail.
    (2) Adam Smith was the most intelligent economist of the eighteenth century.
    (3) Division of labor will improve any nation's standard of living.
    (4) Pins made in factories are better than pins made by hand.
    (5) Division of labor requires specialization among workers.

4. Which workers today best illustrate the concept of division of labor?

    (1) automobile assembly line workers
    (2) members of a rock band
    (3) teachers in an elementary school
    (4) doctors in a hospital
    (5) clerks in a department store

Questions 5 and 6 refer to the following information.

Coral reefs, sometimes called "the rain forests of the sea," support at least a million plant and animal species. They also protect beaches from erosion and attract tourist income. Today, however, the world's coral reefs are in trouble. Since 1997, scientists have been monitoring more than 1,100 coral reefs around the globe. They have recorded damage to coral reefs in places where wastes are dumped into the sea. They have seen coral smothered when fishers have caught too many algae-eating fish. They have noted places where careless boaters and fishers using dynamite have destroyed coral. The news is grim, but most coral reefs can be saved if governments will protect them and work harder to control the factors that threaten them.

5. Which of the following causes coral reef damage?

    (1) a rise in ocean temperatures
    (2) radioactive waste and beach erosion
    (3) pollution and careless fishing practices
    (4) a lack of government protection
    (5) tourism and an overpopulation of fish

6. Which of the following statements is supported by information in the article?

    (1) If coral reefs were to die out, the world's beaches would disappear.
    (2) Fishing in the world's oceans should be banned.
    (3) More species of plants and animals live in coral reefs than in rain forests.
    (4) Coral reefs and algae-eating fish have a mutually supportive relationship.
    (5) Scientists need volunteer help to continue monitoring coral reefs.

Questions 7 and 8 refer to the following political cartoon.

In the cartoon below, the dog is labeled "ISRAEL" and the cat is labeled "PALESTINIANS."

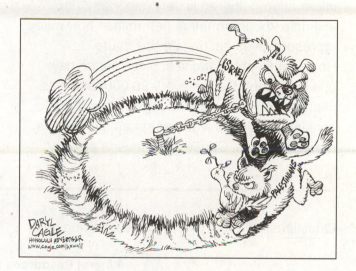

7. Which of the following statements is true about both animals in this cartoon?

    (1) Both would prefer to be friends.
    (2) Secretly, both are enjoying the chase.
    (3) Both show violent tendencies.
    (4) They are both chained in some way.
    (5) If given the chance, both would attack humans.

8. What does the cartoonist imply through this image?

    (1) Israel deserves the chance to solve its problems with its neighbors.
    (2) Dogs and cats should not confined to the same living space.
    (3) The Palestinians are to blame for the problems in the Middle East.
    (4) The Israelis are to blame for the problems in the Middle East.
    (5) Strife between the Palestinians and the Israelis has gone on for some time.

Question 9 refers to the following information.

The Constitution requires that the federal government obtain an accurate count of the population of the United States every ten years. Thus, the government takes a census. The information gathered is very important. For example, the information determines how many representatives each state has in the U.S. House of Representatives. Since states have one representative for every 30,000 residents, changes in population, as reported by the census, determine whether states gain or lose representatives. Census information also determines the amount of federal funds that states receive for education, housing, welfare programs, and other public services.

9. Which statement best summarizes the main idea of this passage?

(1) Taking a census is a constitutional responsibility.
(2) A census is valuable in many ways.
(3) States make use of census data.
(4) Census officials work hard to get an accurate count of the population.
(5) Congressional representation is based on census statistics.

Questions 10 and 11 refer to the following map.

Mineral Resources of the Middle East

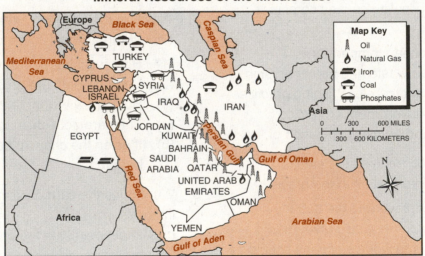

10. Based on a comparison of the countries on the map, which statement is accurate?

(1) Turkey has more oil than Iran does.
(2) Only Oman and Yemen have no natural gas fields.
(3) Syria and Jordan have no oil.
(4) Most of the Middle East's oil is in Iraq.
(5) Lebanon, Israel, and Cyprus have no natural resources.

11. If new technology replaced oil with another source of energy, what prediction about this region would most likely come true?

(1) Several countries would face severe economic problems.
(2) The region would switch from exporting oil to exporting coal and natural gas.
(3) Iran and Iraq would go to war.
(4) Yemen would seize Oman's oil.
(5) These countries would try to acquire the new technology quickly.

Questions 12 and 13 refer to the following photograph of a World War I poster.

12. What values does this poster promote?

    (1) truth and justice
    (2) creativity and respect
    (3) compassion and determination
    (4) freedom and religious faith
    (5) patriotism and equality

13. A poster making a similar appeal today would probably show which of the following?

    (1) a flag but no person
    (2) a person but no flag
    (3) more Asian and Latino names
    (4) soldiers, weapons, and tanks
    (5) children instead of adults

Questions 14 and 15 refer to the following information.

Chief Joseph (1840–1904) was an important leader for the Nez Percé. By the early 1870s, many Nez Percé had been relocated to a reservation. In 1877, however, Chief Joseph fled with a band of Nez Percé to Canada. When federal troops pursued them, the Nez Percé resisted. After four months on the run, they finally surrendered in 1877, and most were sent to a reservation in Oklahoma. Chief Joseph said, "I have carried a heavy load on my back ever since I was a boy. I realized then that we could not hold our own with the white men. We were like deer. They were like grizzly bears." He later made several appeals for the return of his people's land. Even though the government did not grant his request, many officials were impressed by his courage.

14. Which of the following best restates the quotation from Chief Joseph?

    (1) The Nez Percé are one with nature.
    (2) I have lived an unhappy life because I had to leave my home.
    (3) Native Americans are equal to white people in every way.
    (4) For a long time I have known that white men would defeat us.
    (5) White people have no mercy.

15. What was the effect of Chief Joseph's appeals for the return of his people's land?

    (1) The Nez Percé reservation was expanded.
    (2) He gained the respect of many officials.
    (3) The government returned the land.
    (4) The Nez Percé were moved to a reservation in Oklahoma.
    (5) His people regained their hunting rights.

Check your answers on pages 163–164.

Science

Science

Science

Science

The GED Science Test requires you to use critical thinking skills to answer questions about passages and graphics based on topics in life science, physical science, and Earth and space science. Besides developing your critical thinking skills in this unit, you will also work on graphic skills such as reading and interpreting tables, diagrams, and graphs.

Describe a time you have used diagrams to assemble or operate a machine. _____

_____

Describe what you consider a balanced meal.

_____

Thinking About Science

You may not realize how often you use the basics of science and thinking skills in your daily life. Think about your recent activities.

Check the box for each activity you did.

☐ Did you use a radio, flashlight, or other appliance that runs on batteries?

☐ Did you try to solve a problem by eliminating possible causes?

☐ Did you listen to the results of a scientific study about what is good or bad for your health?

☐ Did you get information from posters or pamphlets at a doctor's office?

☐ Did you compare the nutrition information for products at the supermarket?

☐ Did you apply information from a weather report to make plans?

Write some other activities where you used science knowledge or principles.

_____

_____

_____

Previewing the Unit

In this unit, you will learn:

• how to solve problems

• how to think about relationships between things and events

• how to interpret information and draw conclusions

• how to understand and use information from tables, diagrams, and graphs

Lesson 28	The Scientific Method	Lesson 35	Hypothesis
Lesson 29	Restate/Summarize	Lesson 36	Application
Lesson 30	Graphic Skill: Tables	Lesson 37	Graphic Skill: Bar Graphs and Line Graphs
Lesson 31	Sequence of Events		
Lesson 32	Cause/Effect	Lesson 38	Conclusions
Lesson 33	Compare/Contrast	Lesson 39	Adequacy of Data
Lesson 34	Graphic Skill: Diagrams	Lesson 40	Graphic Skill: Circle Graphs

The Scientific Method

The **scientific method** is a series of logical steps that can be used to solve problems. These steps usually include making observations, asking questions, testing ideas, and forming conclusions. On the GED Science Test, you will see questions about the scientific method.

For many years, doctors thought stress and diet caused ulcers. In the 1980s, two Australian doctors noticed that their ulcer patients often had the same bacterium in their stomach. They began to wonder if the bacterium might be causing the ulcers. One of the doctors, Dr. Barry Marshall, figured out how to grow the bacterium in the lab and determined which drugs would kill it. He then tested these drugs on people with ulcers. He found that 70 percent of the ulcers went away in people who used the drugs. Today, almost all ulcers are cured with antibiotic drugs.

TIP

When using the scientific method to approach a problem, try to put the problem in the form of a question.

1. What question did Dr. Marshall and his colleague ask?

   _____

2. How did Dr. Marshall test his idea about the cause of ulcers?

   _____

1. The doctors asked: Does this bacterium cause ulcers? 2. Dr. Marshall determined which drugs would kill the bacterium and tested these drugs on people with ulcers.

To understand and use the scientific method, make a chart like the one below.

OBSERVATIONS What we know	QUESTION What we want to find out	TEST/RESEARCH How we can find out	CONCLUSIONS What we learned
The same bacterium is found in many ulcer patients.	Does the bacterium found in ulcer patients cause ulcers?	Treat ulcer patients with a drug that kills the bacterium.	The bacterium does cause ulcers.

When you read about scientific studies, ask yourself:

- What was the question? How was the question answered or tested?

- What conclusions were drawn?

Think of a time when you looked for an answer to a question. How did you try to find the answer? What were your conclusions?

Read the passage and complete the chart. Then answer the questions.

If you drop a heavy ball and a lightweight ball at the same time from the same height, will one reach the ground before the other? A long time ago, people believed that heavy things fall faster than light things. In the 1600s, Galileo tested this idea. He timed how long it took balls that were the same size but had different weights to fall from a tower. Galileo found that weight did not affect how fast the balls fell to the ground. They reached the ground at the same time.

OBSERVATIONS	QUESTION	TEST/RESEARCH	CONCLUSIONS
People say that heavy things fall faster than light things.		Measure how long it takes heavy and light balls to fall to the ground from a tower.	

1. What question did Galileo investigate?

_____

2. What conclusion did Galileo reach?

_____

GED PRACTICE   **Choose the one best answer to the question.**

Earth is surrounded by an envelope of ozone, which protects us from harmful sunrays. In the 1970s, scientists correctly predicted that a hole would form in the ozone layer.

How was the ozone hole predicted in advance? Scientists noticed that humans were using a large amount of chlorofluorocarbons (CFCs), which are chemicals found in refrigerators and air conditioners. They wanted to know if CFCs would affect the atmosphere, so they tested these chemicals in the lab. At first, the CFCs seemed harmless to the atmosphere. But under the right conditions—the conditions that occur in the upper part of the atmosphere—CFCs break down ozone. Knowing this, the scientists predicted that a hole would form.

3. According to the passage, which question led to the research on CFCs and the atmosphere?

(1) Are CFCs useful in refrigerators and air conditioners?

(2) Why is there an increase in the use of CFCs?

(3) What effect will the ozone hole have on Earth?

(4) What effect do CFCs have on the atmosphere?

(5) How long will it take CFCs to cause a hole in the ozone layer?

Restate/Summarize

Some questions on the GED Science Test will ask you to restate and summarize information. To **restate** information, you repeat it but in a different and often shorter way. When you restate information in a shortened form, you are **summarizing.** Think about the most important points in the paragraph below.

Have you ever heard that carrots are good for your eyesight? It's true. Carrots and other colorful vegetables contain chemicals that help protect your eyes from cataracts and other age-related problems. You get the most benefit from eating spinach, pumpkin, squash, corn, and other green, orange, and yellow vegetables. Red berries are also of benefit. The bright colors indicate the presence of chemicals that are good for eyesight.

TIP

In questions that ask you to summarize, first eliminate any answer choices that are details from the passage. Look for the most important points.

1. Restate why some fruits and vegetables are good for a person's eyesight.

   _____

   _____

2. Summarize the information in the passage.

   _____

   _____

1. Some fruits and vegetables contain chemicals that help protect eyesight.
2. Eating brightly colored fruits and vegetables is good for your eyesight.

To summarize a passage, make a summary chart.

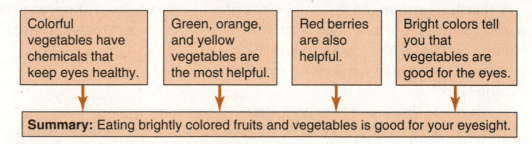

When you restate or summarize scientific information, ask yourself:
- What subject was investigated?
- What conclusion did the researchers reach?

....

Can you remember a time when you retold a story or summarized a movie? How did you decide what information to include or leave out?

Read the passage and complete the chart. Then answer the questions.

What shape is the planet Earth? If you think of a globe, you probably picture a planet shaped like a large beach ball. In fact, Earth is not a perfect ball shape. It has the shape of a ball that has been squashed a little. Earth is flatter near the north and south poles and thicker around the middle along the imaginary line called the equator. This shape is called an oblate spheroid.

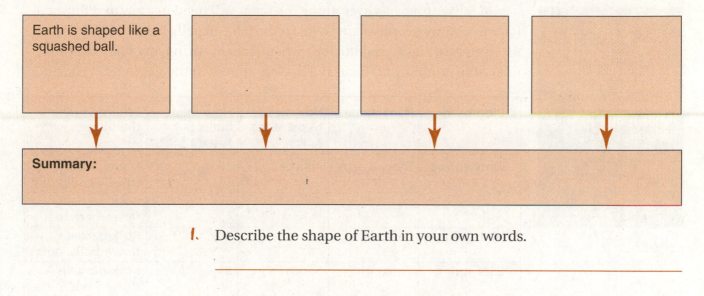

Earth is shaped like a squashed ball.

Summary:

1. Describe the shape of Earth in your own words.

   _____

   _____

2. Summarize the information in the passage.

   _____

   _____

GED PRACTICE **Choose the one best answer to the question.**

People, buildings, computers, and even things you cannot see, such as air, are all made of matter. Light and sound are not matter. Unlike things that are made of matter, light and sound do not take up space. They have no mass and no volume.

There are a little more than 100 different kinds of matter. Each kind of matter is called an element. Elements join together in different ways to make everything in the world. Scientists organize the elements into a chart called the periodic table.

3. Which of the following best summarizes the main point of the first paragraph?

   (1) People, buildings, computers, and air are examples of matter.
   (2) Even though you cannot see it, air has mass and volume.
   (3) Matter is anything that has mass and volume.
   (4) Light and sound have no mass and no volume.
   (5) Light and sound do not take up any space and so cannot be matter.

Tables

A **table** is a type of chart that presents information in rows and columns. Some types of information are easier to understand when shown in a table rather than in a paragraph. The GED Science Test presents different kinds of information in tables. Read the information and look at the table below. Then answer the questions.

A flower bulb has everything the plant will need to grow and flower later on. Many people plant bulbs in the fall—usually before the first frost. All winter the bulbs prepare for spring. Then in spring, the plants sprout out of the ground, and beautiful flowers appear in the garden.

TIP

Look carefully at a table's title and headings. The title tells you what the table is about. The headings of the rows and columns help you find specific information in the table.

Blooms in	Plant name	How deep to plant the bulbs	How many bulbs per square foot	Where to plant the bulbs
Early spring	Snow crocus	4 inches	10	Lawns, under trees, on hills
	Iris	4 inches	6	Rock gardens, flowerbeds, pots
Mid spring	Daffodil	8 inches	4	Rock gardens, flowerbeds, pots
Late spring	Dutch iris	5 inches	8	Rock gardens, flowerbeds, pots
	Late tulip	6 inches	6	Flowerbeds, pots

1. What kind of information does the table present?

_____

2. Summarize the information in the passage and the table.

_____

1. The table gives information about how, when, and where to plant different kinds of bulbs. 2. You can summarize the information like this: Plant fall bulbs according to their specific requirements in order to have beautiful flowers in spring.

When you get information from tables, ask yourself:
- What is the title or topic of the table?

- How is the information in the rows and columns organized?

Think of a time when you used a table for information. What kind of information was it? Did the table make the information easier to understand?

Read the information and look at the table. Then answer the questions.

A suspension is a mixture that has small particles dispersed, or distributed, in another substance. Liquid medicines are often suspensions. Here are some other examples of suspensions.

Name of suspension	Example	Description of suspension
foam	Whipped cream	gas dispersed in liquid
solid foam	Marshmallows	gas dispersed in solid
liquid aerosol	Fog	liquid dispersed in gas
sol	Milk	solid dispersed in liquid
solid sol	Pearls	solid dispersed in solid
smoke	Dust in the air	solid dispersed in gas
emulsion	Mayonnaise	liquid dispersed in liquid
solid emulsion	Butter	liquid dispersed in solid

1. What is the main topic of the table?

   _____

2. Give two examples of foams from the table.

   _____

3. Restate the definition of a suspension.

   _____

   _____

GED PRACTICE   **Choose the one best answer to the question.**

Measuring Earthquakes on the Modified Mercalli Intensity Scale

Levels	Characteristics
1–2	Not felt by people; need special instruments to detect
3	Feels like the vibrations of a truck passing by
4	Windows and doors rattle
5	Walls of buildings crack
6	Damage to buildings
7	Many buildings crumble
8+	Extensive damage

4. According to this table, an earthquake of which level is most likely to damage homes beyond repair?

   (1) 1
   (2) 3
   (3) 4
   (4) 5
   (5) 7

   Check your answers on page 165.

Science Skills Practice 1

Directions: Choose the <u>one best answer</u> to each question.

Questions 1 and 2 refer to the following information.

Some nurses use a therapy called therapeutic touch (TT) to heal patients. These nurses move their hands closely above the patient's body. The TT therapists say they can balance a person's energy fields and help healing.

At the age of 9, Emily Rosa designed an experiment on TT for a science fair. She asked 21 TT therapists to detect her energy field without looking. Rosa set up a screen. She then placed either her left or her right hand through a hole in the screen and just over each therapist's hand. Only 44 percent of the therapists correctly guessed which hand Rosa used. Rosa published the results of her work in the *Journal of the American Medical Association* as evidence that TT practitioners cannot feel energy fields.

1. What question did Rosa's experiment test?

    (1) Does touch therapy work?
    (2) How do touch therapists heal patients?
    (3) How does touch therapy work?
    (4) Can touch therapists feel energy fields?
    (5) Why does touch therapy work?

2. Which of the following best restates Rosa's conclusions?

    (1) Only 44 percent of therapists can heal using touch therapy.
    (2) TT therapists cannot detect energy fields.
    (3) TT therapists can balance a person's energy levels.
    (4) Nurses are better at caring for patients than TT therapists.
    (5) TT therapists are not adequately trained.

Questions 3 and 4 refer to the following table.

Highest Points on Each Continent

Continent	Place	Height (in meters)
Africa	Mt. Kibo	5,895
Antarctica	Vinson Massif	5,139
Asia	Mt. Everest	8,846
Australia	Mt. Kosciusko	2,228
Europe	Mt. El'Brus	5,642
North America	Mt. McKinley	6,194
South America	Mt. Aconcagua	6,960

3. According to the table, which continent has the highest point?

    (1) Africa
    (2) Antarctica
    (3) Asia
    (4) Europe
    (5) North America

4. Which of the following best summarizes the information in the table?

    (1) Asia has more mountains than the other continents do.
    (2) The land on Earth is divided into seven main continents.
    (3) The highest point on each continent is a mountain peak.
    (4) The highest points on each continent vary in height by thousands of meters.
    (5) The highest points on each continent are about the same height.

Questions 5 and 6 refer to the following table.

Golden Corn Flakes Nutrition Facts
Serving Size 1 cup (28g)
Servings Per Container 20

Amount Per Serving	Cereal Only	Cereal with 1/2 cup Fat Free Milk
Calories	100	140
Calories from Fat	0	0
% Daily Value based on a 2,000 calorie diet		
Total Fat 0g	0%	0%
Saturated Fat 0g	0%	0%
Cholesterol 0mg	0%	0%
Sodium 260mg	11%	14%
Potassium 30mg	1%	7%
Total Carbohydrate 24g	8%	10%
Dietary Fiber 1g	4%	4%
Sugars 2g		
Protein 2g		

5. Which of the following best restates the information in the table about the serving size of Golden Corn Flakes?

   (1) One serving has 100 calories.
   (2) There are 20 servings in the box.
   (3) Each serving has 0% fat.
   (4) Each cup of cereal is one serving.
   (5) Milk should be added to the cereal.

6. How might you test if the table accurately reports the amount of cereal in the box?

   (1) Ask the manufacturer.
   (2) Weigh the box of cereal before opening it.
   (3) Measure the number of cups of cereal in the box.
   (4) Measure one cup of cereal with one-half cup of milk.
   (5) Compare the table with one from a different brand of corn flakes.

Questions 7 and 8 refer to the following information.

   The labels inside many clothes recommend dry cleaning. Clothes made of silk or wool can lose their shape or shrink when washed in water. Although dry cleaning does not use water, it is not a dry process. Instead of water, dry cleaning uses a chemical. You can sometimes smell this chemical on clothes when you pick them up from the dry cleaners. One chemical often used in dry cleaning is called tetrachloroethylene. It gets out grease and other stains that are difficult to remove. Tetrachloroethylene is less toxic than some other dry cleaning chemicals and is not flammable.

7. Which of the following is the best summary of the paragraph?

   (1) Dry cleaning is better than regular cleaning because it does not use water.
   (2) It is safer to wash clothes in tetrachloroethylene than in water.
   (3) Tetrachloroethylene is a chemical used for dry cleaning clothes.
   (4) Many silk and wool clothes require dry cleaning.
   (5) In dry cleaning, clothes are washed with a chemical instead of water.

8. Which of the following best restates why tetrachloroethylene is used in dry cleaning?

   (1) It gets rid of stains and is less harmful than some other dry cleaning chemicals.
   (2) It shrinks some fabrics, such as wool.
   (3) It is able to clean clothing without getting it wet.
   (4) Its strong smell lets customers know that their clothes have really been cleaned.
   (5) The labels inside many clothes recommend using this chemical.

Check your answers on page 165.

Sequence of Events

When you **sequence** events, you put them in the order in which they occur. Some questions on the GED Science Test will ask you about the sequence of events. Read the passage below. Then answer the questions.

Marie Curie was born Marya Sklodowska in Poland in 1867. As a young adult, she worked for eight years as a governess to put her sister through school in France. Curie herself moved to France in 1891, where she later graduated first in her class in physics. In 1903, she became the first woman to be awarded an advanced science degree in France. That same year, she received the Nobel Prize for Physics for her work on radioactivity. In 1911, she received a second Nobel Prize, this time in chemistry, for her discovery of two radioactive elements.

1. What did Marie Curie do before going to school in France?

_____

2. What happened the same year that Marie Curie received her advanced degree?

_____

1. She worked as a governess. 2. Curie received the Nobel Prize for Physics.

To identify sequence, make a chart like the one below.

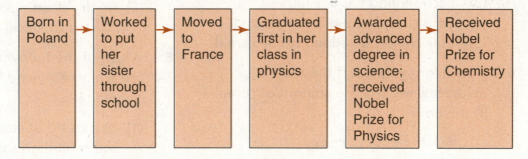

When you identify the sequence of events, ask yourself:

- What clue words help me determine the order of events?

- Does the order of events make sense?

....

Can you remember a time when you gave someone directions? What words did you use to tell the person what to do?

Read the passage and complete the chart. Then answer the questions.

Water continuously cycles between Earth and its atmosphere. Water falls onto Earth in the form of rain, snow, sleet, and other forms of precipitation. Some of this water soaks into the land. Some water flows into lakes and rivers. Plants take in water, too. Next, water returns to the atmosphere by a process called evaporation. Water can evaporate directly from the Earth's surface or through tiny holes in plant leaves. When water evaporates, it changes from a liquid form into a gaseous form called water vapor. In the atmosphere, condensation then occurs. This is the process of water vapor becoming liquid again. When condensation happens, water becomes available to fall back to Earth in the form of precipitation.

The Water Cycle

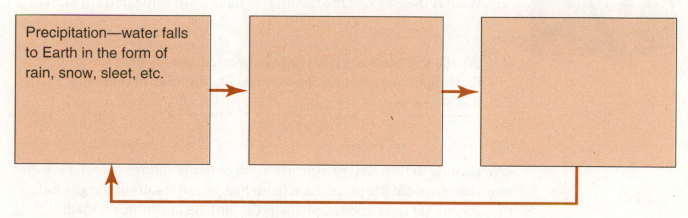

Precipitation—water falls to Earth in the form of rain, snow, sleet, etc.

1. In the water cycle, which step comes after precipitation?

_____

2. Which step comes before precipitation?

_____

GED PRACTICE   **Choose the one best answer to the question.**

A good workout should begin with a warm-up and end with a cool-down. This means that each exercise session begins and ends gradually. To warm up, for example, a jogger might first stretch her muscles and then start jogging at a normal pace. Gradually, she might increase her pace. To cool down at the end of a jog, a jogger could slow to a walk and then gently stretch out her muscles.

3. According to the passage, which of the following is the last step in a good workout?

(1) Jog at a normal pace.
(2) Gradually decrease jogging pace.
(3) Stretch muscles gently.
(4) Warm up your body slowly.
(5) Increase jogging pace.

SEQUENCE OF EVENTS   Check your answers on page 165.

Cause/Effect

On the GED Science Test, you may see questions about cause-and-effect relationships. A **cause** makes something happen. An **effect** is the result of a cause. As you read the passage, think about the cause-and-effect relationships.

TIP

Cause-and-effect relationships are often signaled by words such as *cause, effect, result, because, as a result, led to,* and *caused by.*

Over the past 30 years, the average temperature in Alaska has risen about 7°F. As a result, some places where the ground used to be frozen solid all year long now thaw and soften during the summer. In these areas, trees and telephone poles are sinking or tilting. Roads are caving in. Houses built on permafrost, the permanently frozen layers of soil, are settling. Even parts of the Trans-Alaska Pipeline have begun to sag.

1. What is the cause of the melting permafrost in some parts of Alaska?

_____

2. What are some things that have happened as a result of the ground thawing in places where it used to be frozen solid all year long?

_____

_____

1. According to the passage, warmer average temperatures over the last 30 years have caused the permafrost to melt. 2. Some results of the ground thawing are (1) trees and telephone poles sinking or tilting, (2) roads caving in, (3) houses settling, and (4) the oil pipeline sagging.

To understand cause and effect, make a cause/effect chart. Notice that the effect of a cause may in turn become another cause.

Cause ⟶	Effect
Temperature rises.	Permafrost melts.
Permafrost melts.	Trees, poles, houses, roads and oil pipelines sink and sag.

When you read about cause-and-effect relationships, ask yourself:
- What happened? What caused it to happen?
- What happened as a result?

Think of a time when you accidentally caused something to happen. What did you do? What was the effect?

Read the passage and add one cause and one effect to the chart. Then answer the questions.

Exposure to high temperatures for a long time can cause heat exhaustion, heat stroke, and in some cases, death. Children, the elderly, people with heart disease, and people performing physical activities are most at risk for heat-related illnesses. To

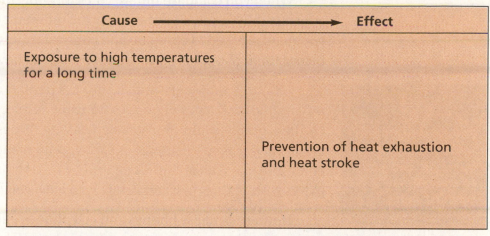

Cause ➡	Effect
Exposure to high temperatures for a long time	
	Prevention of heat exhaustion and heat stroke

prevent heat-related illnesses, stay cool. Spend time in air-conditioned places, even if only for a few minutes at a time. Reduce your activities. Plan outdoor activities at a cooler time of day. Take cool showers. Make sure to drink plenty of water.

1. What might cause a person to suffer heat exhaustion or heat stroke?

_____

2. What are some ways to prevent heat-related illnesses?

_____

GED PRACTICE Choose the one best answer to the question.

When you pull a sweater over your head on a winter day, does you hair stick up? If so, your hair and the sweater have become electrically charged by the movement of the sweater over your hair. Because your hair and your sweater have different electric charges, they are attracted to one another. Opposite charges attract.

There are two kinds of charges: positive and negative. Rubbing a balloon across your hair gives your hair a positive charge and the balloon a negative charge.

Like charges repel. For example, if you rub two balloons across your hair, both balloons will be attracted to your hair. Both balloons will have the same electric charge. However, the balloons will push away from each other. That is because like charges repel each other.

3. According to the passage, two balloons that have been rubbed across a person's hair will repel one another. What causes them to repel?

(1) The balloons have opposite charges.
(2) The balloons have like charges.
(3) Both balloons are made of rubber.
(4) Both balloons have lost their electric charges.
(5) The balloons now have hair-care products on them.

   Check your answers on page 166.

Compare/Contrast

When you **compare** things, you show how they are alike. When you **contrast** things, you show how they are different. On the GED Science Test, you may be asked to compare and contrast things. As you read the passage below, think about how things are similar and how they are different.

Although they look similar, cordless phones and cell phones work differently. Both types of phones transmit and receive radio waves. A cordless phone communicates signals with its base, which in turn sends and receives signals using a regular telephone line. Cellular phones communicate with antennas on towers and tall buildings. An antenna works with phones in a certain area, called a cell.

1. How are cordless phones and cell phones alike?

   _____

   _____

2. How are cordless phones and cell phones different?

   _____

   _____

1. They look similar and both transmit and receive radio waves. 2. A cordless phone communicates signals with its base, which sends signals using a regular telephone line. In contrast, cellular phones communicate with antennas on towers and tall buildings.

To compare and contrast two things, use a Venn diagram. Write the similarities in the overlap. Write the differences in the individual circles.

Cell phones
Send and receive signals using antennas on tall buildings

Both
Look similar
Transmit and receive radio waves

Cordless phones
Communicate with a base, which sends and receives signals using a regular telephone line

When you compare and contrast things, ask yourself:

- Am I being asked to compare or contrast?

- How are the things alike or different?

Have you ever replaced a pair of sneakers, a television set, or a cell phone with a newer model? What did the two things have in common? How were they different?

Read the passage and complete the Venn diagram. Then answer the questions.

Bacteria and viruses are two kinds of germs. Both are very tiny and cause disease, but bacteria are living cells. Like other living things, bacteria can reproduce themselves. Viruses are inert particles. To replicate, they must enter a host cell. Viruses can replicate inside cells because they use the same genetic instructions as other life forms. In fact, viruses and bacteria contain genetic material made of similar chemicals, and they both can evolve over time. These similarities have led scientists to believe that viruses are particles left over from cell ancestors.

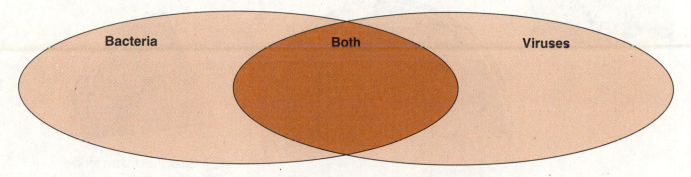

1. How are bacteria and viruses alike?

_____

_____

2. How are bacteria and viruses different?

_____

_____

GED PRACTICE Choose the <u>one best answer</u> to the question.

The numbers on the bottom of plastic containers are recycling codes, ranging from 1 to 6. Most recycling programs accept plastics coded 1 and 2, but many do not take the others.

Plastics coded 1 are polyethylene terephthalate or PET plastics. You find PET in soda bottles and electrical insulation. PET can be recycled into backpacks, carpet, and new plastic bottles. Plastics coded 2 are high-density polyethylene, or HDPE. Milk jugs, bleach bottles, and plastic grocery sacks are made of HDPE. When recycled, HDPE can be used to make furniture, toys, trashcans, and fences.

3. According to the passage, how are PET and HDPE plastics similar?

They are both

(1) found in milk jugs
(2) used to make plastic grocery sacks
(3) marked with recycling code 1
(4) commonly recycled into new products
(5) used in electrical insulation

COMPARE/CONTRAST

Check your answers on page 166. **111**

Diagrams

Diagrams are drawings of an object, concept, or process. The GED Science Test will include one or more diagrams. Read the information and look at the diagram below. Then answer the questions that follow.

Temperatures increase as one digs deeper into Earth. The thin outer layer of Earth can get as hot as 347°F. The center of Earth is as hot as the sun's surface—more than 10,800°F.

TIP

When you see a science diagram, "picture" the real object or process in your mind.

Inside Earth

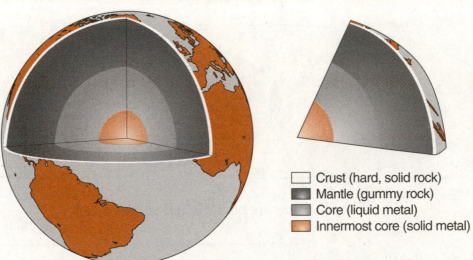

☐ Crust (hard, solid rock)
■ Mantle (gummy rock)
▦ Core (liquid metal)
▨ Innermost core (solid metal)

1. Look at the title. What is the topic of the diagram?

   _____

2. Look at the key. To drill a hole to the center of Earth, in which sequence would you encounter each of Earth's layers?

   _____

   _____

1. The diagram shows the layers inside Earth. 2. You would encounter the layers in this order: crust, mantle, core, and innermost core.

When you get information from diagrams, ask yourself:

● What is the title or topic of the diagram?

● What do the labels and key point out?

⋯⋯⋯⋯⋯⋯⋯⋯⋯⋯⋯⋯⋯⋯⋯⋯⋯⋯⋯⋯⋯⋯⋯⋯⋯⋯⋯⋯⋯⋯⋯

Think of a time when you used a diagram to make or learn about something. Was the diagram clear or confusing? Did having a diagram make the task easier?

Read the information and look at the diagram. Then answer the questions.

The diagram below shows two different breakfasts. One is recommended by the U.S. Department of Agriculture (USDA). One is based on a currently popular high protein, low carbohydrate diet.

USDA Breakfast

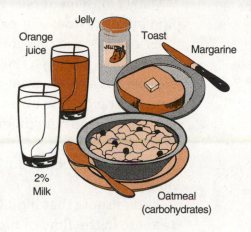

- Jelly
- Orange juice
- Toast
- Margarine
- 2% Milk
- Oatmeal (carbohydrates)

High Protein, Low Carbohydrate Breakfast

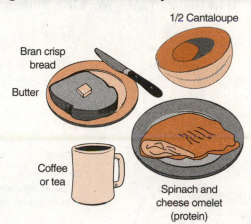

- 1/2 Cantaloupe
- Bran crisp bread
- Butter
- Coffee or tea
- Spinach and cheese omelet (protein)

1. What is this diagram about?

_____

2. How does each breakfast introduce fruit into the diet?

_____

_____

3. What is the difference between the two main dishes in the breakfasts?

_____

_____

GED PRACTICE Choose the <u>one best answer</u> to the question.

How Photocopies Are Made

1. The image to be copied is focused on drum.
2. Toner is attracted to image area on the drum.
3. The image on the drum is transferred to paper.
4. Heat fixes the image onto paper.

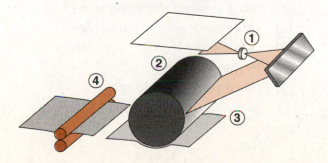

4. What happens after the toner is applied to the image on the drum?

(1) Paper is inserted in the feed tray.
(2) The original image is scanned.
(3) The image is projected on the drum.
(4) The image is transferred to paper.
(5) The image is fixed onto the paper.

Science Skills Practice 2

Directions: Choose the <u>one best answer</u> to each question.

Questions 1 and 2 refer to the following diagram.

How Ballast Tanks Work in a Submarine

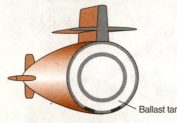

1. Floating: Valves closed; ballast tanks full of air

Ballast tank

2. Diving: Valves open; tanks fill with water

3. Surfacing: Air pumped into tanks; water forced out

1. What is the topic of this diagram?

    (1) military uses of submarines
    (2) how submarines withstand pressure
    (3) how a submarine dives and rises
    (4) sources of air on a submarine
    (5) structure of a ballast tank

2. A submarine captain would order which of the following actions to cause the submarine to rise to the surface?

    The captain would order the crew to

    (1) open the hatch
    (2) pump air into the ballast tanks
    (3) open the valves of the ballast tanks
    (4) let water into the ballast tanks
    (5) increase propeller speed

Questions 3 and 4 refer to the following information.

   Many amusement parks now have new, high intensity rides. For example, some newer roller coasters use rocket motors to increase acceleration. During a ride, your body experiences a much greater than normal force of gravity. The normal G-force of gravity is 1-G, but some new roller coasters can reach G-forces of 5-G and 6-G. That's more than astronauts experience during a space shuttle launch.

   Studies show that high G-forces cause a decrease in the flow of blood to the brain. In extreme cases, the person loses consciousness. Bleeding and stroke can also occur.

3. How do the G-forces of the new roller coasters compare to normal G-force?

    G-forces of the new roller coasters are

    (1) many times greater than normal G-force
    (2) much safer than normal G-force
    (3) about the same as normal G-force
    (4) slightly less than normal G-force
    (5) about the same as a space shuttle launch

4. New Jersey is planning to set a limit on the G-forces of amusement park rides.

    Based on the information in the passage, New Jersey is trying to provide

    (1) more intense, thrilling rides
    (2) safer amusement park rides
    (3) safer space shuttle launches
    (4) higher G-forces
    (5) more powerful rides

Questions 5 through 7 refer to the following information and diagram.

From Earth, the moon can look like a shiny disk. Over a period of 29.5 days, the moon's appearance from Earth changes. During some months, there are two full moons. A second full moon in one month is called a Blue Moon.

The Moon's Eight Phases

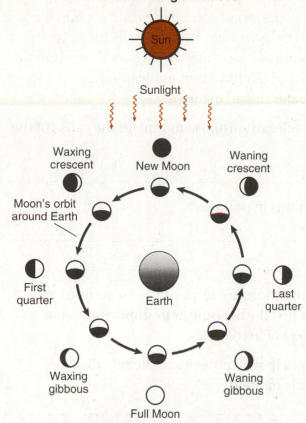

5. Which phase comes just before a full moon?

   (1) waning crescent
   (2) waxing crescent
   (3) first quarter
   (4) waxing gibbous
   (5) waning gibbous

6. Which phase of the moon would appear first in a month with a blue moon?

   (1) new moon
   (2) full moon
   (3) blue moon
   (4) last quarter
   (5) waning gibbous

7. Which phase comes just after a blue moon?

   (1) waning crescent
   (2) first quarter
   (3) last quarter
   (4) waxing gibbous
   (5) waning gibbous

Question 8 refers to the following information.

In diamonds, carbon atoms are arranged in a lattice. In graphite, carbon atoms are arranged in layers. In charcoal, carbon atoms are arranged irregularly.

8. In what way are diamonds, graphite, and charcoal similar?

   The atoms

   (1) are arranged in a lattice
   (2) are arranged in layers
   (3) are arranged irregularly
   (4) consist of carbon
   (5) consist of layers and lattices

Question 9 refers to the following information.

When a choking victim is a baby or toddler, the infant should be seated on the rescuer's lap or placed face up on a flat surface. The rescuer puts the pads of the index and middle fingers under the diaphragm where the chest bone ends. The rescuer presses upward, gently but quickly, to remove the item blocking the baby's windpipe.

9. What is the last step a rescuer should take?

   (1) place two fingers below the diaphragm
   (2) press upward quickly but gently
   (3) place the baby on a flat surface
   (4) pat the baby on the back
   (5) sit the baby on his or her lap

Check your answers on pages 166–167.

Hypothesis

Some of the questions on the GED Science Test explore hypotheses. A **hypothesis** is a possible explanation for something that can be tested by experimentation. Read the passage below. Then answer the questions.

Over the past decade, there has been an increased number of sightings of frogs with extra legs and other deformities. The cause of these deformities is unclear. One scientist hypothesized that parasites called trematodes are responsible in some cases. Trematodes burrow into the skin of young frogs near the place where the hind legs normally form. To imitate the effect of trematodes, the scientist implanted small plastic beads in the same place in young frogs that did not have trematodes. Some of the frogs with the implanted beads also developed extra legs.

1. What hypothesis did the scientist propose to explain the cause of the deformities?

   _____

2. How did the scientist test this hypothesis?

   _____

   _____

1. The hypothesis was that trematodes are responsible for some of the deformities. 2. The scientist tested the hypothesis by implanting small plastic beads to imitate the effect of trematodes.

Drawing a flow map may help you understand the role that hypotheses play in the scientific method.

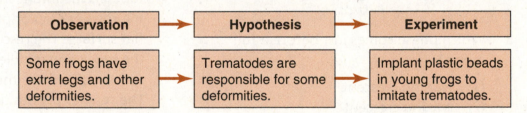

Observation	Hypothesis	Experiment
Some frogs have extra legs and other deformities.	Trematodes are responsible for some deformities.	Implant plastic beads in young frogs to imitate trematodes.

When you read about observations in science, ask yourself:
- What hypothesis was proposed to explain those observations?
- How was that hypothesis tested?

Can you remember a time when you developed a possible explanation for something you saw or heard? How did you test your explanation?

SKILL PRACTICE   Read the passage and complete the flow map. Then answer the questions.

Something is causing boulders to slide across the surface of a dry lakebed in Death Valley National Park. As they slide, the boulders leave furrows in the ground behind them. Some researchers hypothesized that strong winds push the boulders along the lakebed. The researchers carefully measured the direction of the furrows. They found that most of the rocks are moving toward the north-northeast. That is the same direction as the prevailing winds that blow over the lakebed.

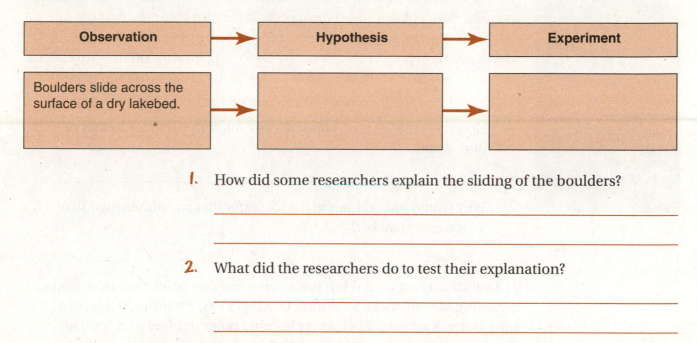

Observation	Hypothesis	Experiment
Boulders slide across the surface of a dry lakebed.		

1. How did some researchers explain the sliding of the boulders?

_____

_____

2. What did the researchers do to test their explanation?

_____

_____

GED PRACTICE   Choose the one best answer to the question.

In 1998, a 10-mile-long oil slick was discovered off the California coast. The oil polluted beaches and killed marine birds and other wildlife. Federal and state officials were determined to find the source of the oil. They hypothesized that the oil came from a ship called the *T/S Command,* which was seen in the vicinity just before the oil slick appeared. The officials analyzed the chemical composition of the oil from the slick and compared it to the composition of oil taken from the *T/S Command.* The oil slick matched the oil from the ship, supporting the officials' hypothesis and providing evidence for the trial. The ship's captain eventually pled guilty to illegally dumping oil and was fined.

3. Which observation led to the hypothesis that the oil in the slick came from the *T/S Command?*

(1) The oil slick was 10 miles long and located off the California coast.
(2) Marine birds and other wildlife were killed by the oil slick.
(3) The *T/S Command* was in the vicinity just before the slick appeared.
(4) Oil from the slick had the same chemical composition as oil from the *T/S Command.*
(5) The captain of the *T/S Command* was put on trial for dumping oil.

Application

The GED Science Test has questions that involve the **application** of ideas. When you apply ideas to a new context, you take information from one situation and use it in another situation. Read the passage below. Then answer the questions.

In areas that get a lot of snow, de-icers are often used to keep roads ice free. The de-icer that is used most often is sodium chloride, or table salt. Other substances, such as calcium chloride and potassium chloride, are used in some areas. De-icers work by dissolving in snow on the ground and forming a solution. The solution has a lower freezing point than pure water. As a result, the solution works to keep the roads from icing over.

1. How does the freezing point of a salt solution compare to that of pure water?

   _____

2. Why would you add salt to the ice water that surrounds the tub of an ice-cream maker?

   _____

1. A solution of water and salt has a lower freezing point than pure water.
2. Adding salt will make a solution that has a lower freezing point than pure water. Ice-cream has a lower freezing point than water does. The ice-water-salt mixture will be colder than ice water alone and will freeze the ice-cream.

Draw a diagram like the one below to apply ideas to new contexts.

Context in passage: De-icers dissolve in the snow on the ground and form a solution that has a lower freezing point than pure water. This keeps roads from icing over.	→	**Idea:** A solution of salt and water has a lower freezing point than pure water.	→	**New context:** Adding salt to the ice water that surrounds the tub of an ice-cream maker will lower the freezing point of the ice water and freeze the ice-cream.

When you read about ideas in science, ask yourself:
- What ideas are being explained?
- What other situations might these ideas apply to?

Did you ever use a tool or gadget for the first time without instructions? Were you able to apply what you already knew about other devices to help you use it?

SKILL PRACTICE   Read the passage and complete the diagram. Then answer the questions.

Overusing a muscle can cause it to become fatigued. However, some muscles are more resistant to fatigue than others. Muscles in the back and legs that help maintain posture and support the body's weight fatigue slowly. In contrast, muscles specialized for producing fast, forceful movements fatigue quickly. Arm muscles that are used to lift heavy objects are examples of quickly fatiguing muscles.

1. What kinds of muscles fatigue slowly?

2. Neck muscles keep the head upright. How do these muscles fatigue? Explain.

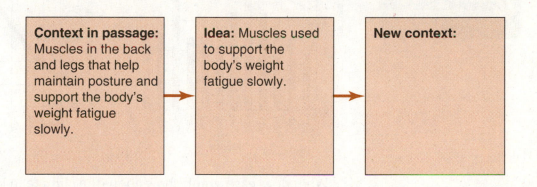

Context in passage: Muscles in the back and legs that help maintain posture and support the body's weight fatigue slowly.

Idea: Muscles used to support the body's weight fatigue slowly.

New context:

GED PRACTICE   Choose the one best answer to the question.

Hurricanes are powerful windstorms. The strength of a hurricane is rated from 1 to 5 based on wind speed. The weakest hurricanes, category 1, have wind speeds of 74–95 miles per hour. They usually cause little or no damage to buildings, except for unanchored mobile homes. They may flood some coastal roads and cause minor damage to piers and poorly built signs. The most powerful hurricanes, category 5, have wind speeds greater than 155 miles per hour. They produce severe damage to windows, doors, and roofs on many buildings. Mobile homes and some other buildings are completely destroyed. Category 5 hurricanes blow down all shrubs, trees, and signs.

3. Tornadoes are another type of violent windstorm. They often have wind speeds of more than 300 miles per hour.

Based on the information in the passage, what is the most likely effect of a direct hit by a tornado?

(1) little or no damage to any buildings
(2) damage to trees and signs
(3) damage to poorly built houses
(4) destruction of buildings and trees
(5) little or no damage to shrubs or trees

APPLICATION

Check your answers on page 167.   **119**

Bar Graphs and Line Graphs

The GED Science Test has questions that require you to read and interpret bar graphs and line graphs. A **bar graph** compares data using bars of various lengths. A **line graph** shows data as a series of points connected by a line. Read the information and look at the graphs below. Then answer the questions that follow.

The kinds of plants that will survive in your garden depend on the climate in your area. These graphs show how two measures of climate vary throughout the year in Dallas, Texas.

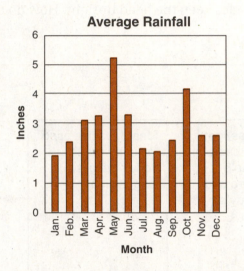

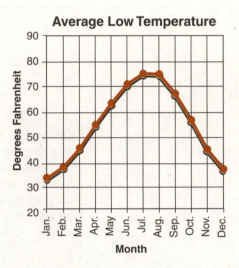

> **TIP**
>
> To find the value of a point on a line graph or a bar in a bar graph, trace a line from the point or the top of the bar to the scale on the left or right side of the graph.

1. What does each graph show about the climate in Dallas?

_____

2. During which month does Dallas receive the most rain?

_____

1. The bar graph shows the average rainfall each month and the line graph shows the average low temperature each month. 2. Dallas receives the most rain in May. In the bar graph, the bar for May is higher than any other bar.

When you interpret a bar graph or line graph, ask yourself:
* What is the title or topic of the graph?
* What information is given along the sides and bottom of the graph?

Think of a time when you saw a bar graph or line graph in a newspaper or magazine. What information did the graph show? Did the graph make it easier to understand the information?

Read the information and look at the graph. Then answer the questions.

All foods contain energy, but the amount of energy in different kinds of foods varies greatly. The energy content of foods is usually measured in calories.

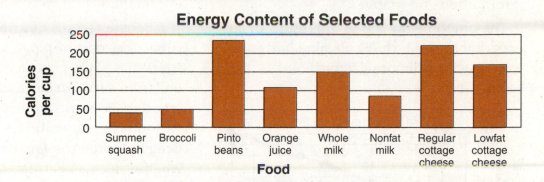

Energy Content of Selected Foods

1. What does this graph show?

   _____

2. How many calories are in one cup of broccoli?

   _____

3. Which food likely contains fewer calories—regular yogurt or nonfat yogurt?

   _____

GED PRACTICE **Choose the one best answer to the question.**

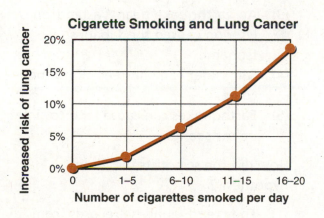

Cigarette Smoking and Lung Cancer

4. Which hypothesis is supported by the information in this graph?

   (1) Smoking cigarettes causes more lung cancer than other forms of smoking.
   (2) Smoking cigarettes increases the risk of getting lung cancer.
   (3) The length of time people smoke increases their risk of getting lung cancer.
   (4) Smoking is not related to the risk of getting lung cancer.
   (5) People are more likely to begin smoking cigarettes after they get lung cancer.

Science Skills Practice 3

Directions: Choose the <u>one best answer</u> to each question.

Questions 1 and 2 refer to the following information and graph.

The graph below shows the results of an experiment in which AA alkaline batteries were used continuously at different temperatures.

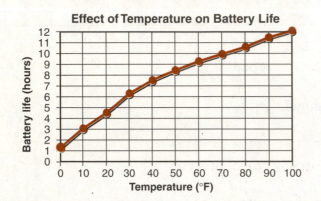

Effect of Temperature on Battery Life

1. Which statement summarizes the results presented in the graph?

   (1) Battery life decreases as temperature decreases.
   (2) Battery life increases as temperature decreases.
   (3) Temperature has no effect on battery life.
   (4) AA batteries last longer than other sizes of batteries.
   (5) Alkaline batteries last longer than other types of batteries.

2. Which statement applies the results of this experiment to another situation?

   (1) Batteries can be stored in a refrigerator.
   (2) Batteries corrode metal when they leak.
   (3) Some batteries can be recharged.
   (4) Flashlights work longer in warm weather.
   (5) Plastic becomes brittle when it is cold.

Questions 3 and 4 refer to the following information.

Japanese records describe a tsunami that struck the coast of Japan in January 1700. A tsunami is a giant ocean wave caused by an undersea earthquake, landslide, or volcanic eruption. Scientists proposed that a large earthquake that occurred near Washington or Oregon caused the Japanese tsunami. To test whether such an earthquake occurred, scientists studied the growth rings of old, dead trees along the Washington coast. The trees had been killed by salt water when the land where they were growing sank below sea level. The scientists found that all of the trees died between 1699 and 1700. This finding supported the idea that there was a large earthquake in the area in 1700.

3. What hypothesis did the scientists test?

   (1) A tsunami struck the coast of Japan in 1700.
   (2) A tsunami is an ocean wave.
   (3) An earthquake near Washington or Oregon caused the Japanese tsunami.
   (4) Salt water can kill trees along the coast.
   (5) Earthquakes can cause land to sink below sea level.

4. How did the scientists test their hypothesis?

   (1) They read Japanese records from 1700.
   (2) They placed trees in saltwater.
   (3) They studied undersea earthquakes.
   (4) They killed trees along the Washington coast.
   (5) They studied the growth rings of old, dead trees.

Questions 5 and 6 refer to the following information and graph.

A scientist tested four household cleaners for their ability to kill bacteria. Cleaners A and B contained antibiotics. Cleaners C and D did not. The results are shown in the graph below.

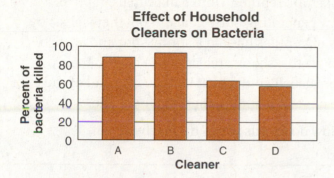

Effect of Household Cleaners on Bacteria

5. What hypothesis did the scientist test?

(1) Bacteria are resistant to most antibiotics.
(2) Cleaners with antibiotics are used more than other cleaners.
(3) Most household cleaners contain bacteria.
(4) Cleaners with antibiotics are more effective at killing bacteria.
(5) Household cleaners come in several varieties.

6. Which of the following restates a result shown in the graph?

(1) There was no difference in the ability of the cleaners to kill bacteria.
(2) Cleaners with antibiotics were most effective at killing bacteria.
(3) Cleaners C and D were most effective at killing bacteria.
(4) Cleaner C killed the most bacteria.
(5) Less than half of the bacteria were killed by any of the cleaners tested.

Question 7 refers to the following information.

Sunlight can be converted directly into electricity through the photovoltaic process. In this process, light is absorbed by a thin layer of silicon or a similar material. The absorbed light causes electrons to move through the material, producing an electric current. The photovoltaic process is often used to supply electricity to devices that cannot be connected to power lines, such as satellites and buoys.

7. Which device involves an application of the photovoltaic process?

(1) a corded telephone
(2) a solar-powered calculator
(3) a remote-control light switch
(4) a battery-powered cell phone
(5) a battery-powered laptop computer

Question 8 refers to the following information.

Metamorphosis is a process in which some young animals change their form and function as they become adults. The changing of a caterpillar into a butterfly is an example of metamorphosis. The caterpillar has a wormlike body and eats leaves. It becomes an adult butterfly that has wings and drinks nectar.

8. Which of the following is an application of metamorphosis in another animal?

(1) the growth of a puppy into an adult dog
(2) the changing of fur color from brown to gray on an old dog
(3) the development of a legless, fishlike tadpole into a frog
(4) the changing of color by a chameleon to blend with its surroundings
(5) the shedding of skin by a snake as it grows

Conclusions

Some questions on the GED Science Test ask you to draw conclusions based on information in a passage, diagram, or graph. A **conclusion** is a statement that follows logically from certain facts. Read the passage below. Then answer the questions.

People who have snakes as pets must take care to keep their pets at the right temperature. Snakes are reptiles. Unlike mammals, reptiles cannot warm themselves by generating body heat or cool themselves by sweating. To become warmer, reptiles bask in a sunny spot and absorb heat. To cool down, they move to a shady area and lose heat to their surroundings. Snake owners usually put a heat lamp at one end of the cage for basking and some type of shelter at the other end for shade.

1. Lizards are reptiles. How do lizards warm themselves?

   _____

2. Hamsters are mammals. How do hamsters warm themselves?

   _____

1. Because lizards are reptiles, you can conclude that lizards warm themselves by basking in a sunny spot and absorbing heat. 2. Because hamsters are mammals, you can conclude that hamsters warm themselves by generating body heat.

To draw conclusions, make an If/Then chart. In the *If* column, list facts that are given in a passage or question. In the *Then* column, write a conclusion that can be drawn from those facts.

If	Then
1. Reptiles warm themselves by basking in a sunny spot and absorbing heat. 2. Lizards are reptiles.	Lizards warm themselves by basking in a sunny spot and absorbing heat.
1. Mammals warm themselves by generating body heat. 2. Hamsters are mammals.	Hamsters warm themselves by generating body heat.

When you read about facts in science, ask yourself:
- What logical connection exists between certain facts?
- What conclusion can be drawn from these connected facts?

Think of a time when you used logic to draw a conclusion about something you observed. What did you observe? What conclusion did you draw?

Read the passage and complete the chart by filling in the *Then* column. Then answer the questions.

The walls of the Grand Canyon in Arizona are made of nine layers of very old rock. The layers are arranged in order of their age. The layer at the top of the canyon, called the Kaibab limestone, is the youngest. It formed between 225 million and 280 million years ago. The layer at the bottom is called the Tapeats sandstone. It formed between 500 million and 570 million years ago. Some of the layers between the top and bottom include the Hermit shale, Redwall limestone, and Bright Angel shale.

If	Then
1. The layers are arranged in order of their age.	The Redwall limestone is
2. The layer at the top is the youngest.	
3. The Redwall limestone is below the Kaibab limestone.	

1. What can you conclude about the age of the Redwall limestone compared to the age of the Kaibab limestone?

   _____

2. How many years ago did the Redwall limestone form?

   _____

GED PRACTICE   Choose the one best answer to the question.

Many shortwave radio operators use their radios to talk to people around the world. Shortwave radio waves are electromagnetic waves that have wavelengths of 10 to 100 meters. Other kinds of electromagnetic waves are used for television and FM radio broadcasts. They have wavelengths between 0.1 and 10 meters.

Electromagnetic waves with wavelengths of 10 meters or longer can bounce off a part of the atmosphere called the ionosphere. This allows shortwave radio waves to travel great distances and reach people on the other side of the world. Electromagnetic waves that have wavelengths less than 10 meters simply pass through the ionosphere.

3. Which of the following is a conclusion that can be drawn from the passage?

   (1) Television signals can travel around the world.
   (2) Shortwave radio waves are not electromagnetic waves.
   (3) Shortwave radio waves pass through the ionosphere.
   (4) FM radio waves pass through the ionosphere.
   (5) Television waves bounce off the ionosphere.

   Check your answers on page 168.

Adequacy of Data

For some of the questions on the GED Science Test, you must decide whether data are **adequate,** or sufficient, to support a given statement or conclusion. Read the passage below. Then answer the questions.

For more than 70 years, scientists have known that fluoride is important for healthy teeth. Fluoride is a chemical found naturally in some water supplies. It helps teeth replace minerals that are lost when acids made by bacteria attack the teeth. Children who drink water containing fluoride have up to 70 percent less tooth decay than children who drink water containing no fluoride. In adults, fluoride protects exposed tooth roots along the gums. For these reasons, many communities add fluoride to their water supplies.

1. Does the data in the passage verify the conclusion that fluoride cures cavities? Explain.

_____

2. What data supports the conclusion that fluoride is important for healthy teeth?

_____

1. Scientists have concluded that fluoride helps prevent cavities, but no evidence is presented that it will cure cavities. 2. Fluoride helps teeth replace minerals, children who drink water containing fluoride have up to 70% less tooth decay, and fluoride protects exposed tooth roots along the gums.

To decide if data are adequate to support a conclusion, make a chart. First write the conclusion. Then list all the data that support it.

Conclusion	Fluoride is important for healthy teeth.
Supporting data	1. Fluoride helps teeth replace minerals. 2. Children who drink water containing fluoride have up to 70 percent less tooth decay. 3. Fluoride protects exposed tooth roots along the gums.

When you read about data and conclusions in science, ask yourself:
* What conclusions are being drawn?
* Are there facts to support or contradict the conclusions?

....

Have you ever read a mystery story and solved the mystery before the end? How did you arrive at your conclusion?

Many pots and pans are made out of aluminum or copper. Both metals conduct heat very well, so they heat food quickly. The handles of cookware are often made of plastics called phenolics. Phenolics retain their shape at temperatures up to about 350°F. As a result, the part of the handle that is attached to a metal pan will not melt when the pan is heated on a stove. Phenolics are poor heat conductors, so the part of the handle you touch stays cool during stovetop use.

Conclusion	
Supporting data	1. Phenolics retain shape at high temperatures. 2. Phenolics are poor heat conductors.

1. What conclusion about phenolics can you draw from this passage?

_____

2. Is there enough data in the passage to verify the conclusion that aluminum and copper pans are convenient and long lasting? Explain.

_____

_____

GED PRACTICE   Choose the <u>one best answer</u> to the question.

A glacier is a large mass of ice that moves slowly over the land. During the last Ice Age, a huge glacier covered much of the Upper Midwest. This area includes parts of what are now Wisconsin, Minnesota, and the Dakotas. The glacier disappeared about 10,000 years ago, but evidence of the glacier remains in the present-day landscape. The gently rolling plains in this area are made of finely ground rock and gravel deposited by the glacier. The hills consist of rocks and boulders left behind as the glacier retreated. Shallow depressions formed where large blocks of buried glacier ice melted. Many small lakes now exist where these depressions filled with water.

3. Which fact supports the conclusion that a glacier covered much of the Upper Midwest during the last Ice Age?

(1) The plains in the area are made of rock and gravel.
(2) A glacier is a large mass of ice that moves slowly.
(3) The Upper Midwest includes parts of the Dakotas.
(4) The glacier disappeared about 10,000 years ago.
(5) Many rivers cut through the plains of the Upper Midwest.

Lesson 40

GRAPHIC SKILL

Circle Graphs

You will find questions on the GED Science Test that include circle graphs. A **circle graph** is a circle divided into sections showing the parts that make up a whole. Read the information and look at the circle graph below. Then answer the questions.

Most of the energy used throughout the world comes from fossil fuels. Fossil fuels include petroleum, coal, and natural gas. Other sources of energy include nuclear, hydroelectric, and solar energy.

TIP

Notice that all the sections in a circle graph add up to 100 percent. The biggest section represents the largest percentage of the total.

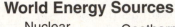

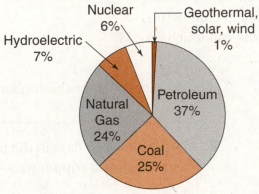

World Energy Sources

Nuclear 6%
Geothermal, solar, wind 1%
Hydroelectric 7%
Natural Gas 24%
Petroleum 37%
Coal 25%

1. What does this circle graph show?

_____

2. What is the largest source of energy in the world?

_____

1. The title indicates that this circle graph shows world energy sources.

2. Petroleum is the largest source of energy in the world. You can see that the section labeled *Petroleum* is larger than any of the other sections. Petroleum's percentage (37%) is greater than any of the other percentages on the graph.

When you interpret a circle graph, ask yourself:

● What is the title or topic of the graph?

● What does each section in the graph represent?

Have you ever sliced a pie into several pieces of different sizes? The slices are parts of the whole pie, like the sections are parts of the whole circle graph. For this reason, circle graphs are sometimes called pie graphs.

Read the information and look at the graph. Then answer the questions.

Diabetes is a disease that causes people to have too much sugar in their blood. People with diabetes can control the disease by injecting themselves with insulin or by taking oral medicines.

Medicines Used by People with Diabetes

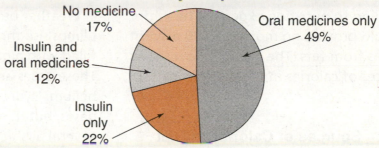

No medicine 17%

Insulin and oral medicines 12%

Insulin only 22%

Oral medicines only 49%

1. What does this graph show?

_____

2. What percentage of people with diabetes use insulin only?

_____

3. What conclusion is supported by the data in the graph?

a. Most people with diabetes take some type of medicine.

b. Insulin is better for controlling diabetes than other medicines.

GED PRACTICE **Choose the <u>one best answer</u> to the question.**

Compared with Mars' atmosphere, Earth's atmosphere is made up of nitrogen (78.1%), oxygen (20.9%), argon (0.9%), and carbon dioxide and other gases (0.1%). Certain bacteria and plants depend on nitrogen. Humans and other animals require oxygen to live. Almost all plants take in carbon dioxide and give off oxygen.

Composition of Mars' Atmosphere

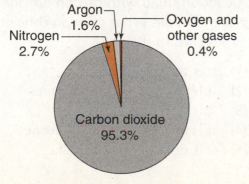

Argon 1.6%

Nitrogen 2.7%

Oxygen and other gases 0.4%

Carbon dioxide 95.3%

4. Which fact presented in the graph supports the conclusion that humans cannot breathe on Mars?

(1) The atmosphere is too thin.

(2) The atmospheric pressure is too low.

(3) The atmosphere does not contain nitrogen.

(4) The atmosphere contains very little carbon dioxide.

(5) The atmosphere contains very little oxygen.

Science Skills Practice 4

Directions: Choose the <u>one best answer</u> to each question.

<u>Questions 1 and 2</u> refer to the following information and graph.

According to nutrition experts, a healthful diet should provide no more than 30 percent of calories from fats. The graph below shows the sources of calories in the diet of one person.

Sources of Calories in Diet

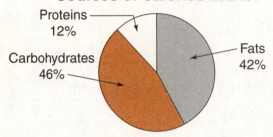

Proteins 12%
Carbohydrates 46%
Fats 42%

1. Which of the following restates a fact about the diet presented in the graph?

   (1) The diet provides too many calories.
   (2) The diet provides too few calories.
   (3) Carbohydrates provide the most calories.
   (4) Proteins provide the most calories.
   (5) Fats provide the fewest calories.

2. What conclusion can be drawn from the data given in the graph?

   (1) The diet contains a healthful balance of carbohydrates, proteins, and fats.
   (2) The person is overweight and should lose weight for better health.
   (3) The diet agrees with nutrition experts' recommendation for protein intake.
   (4) The diet does not meet nutrition experts' recommendation for a healthful diet.
   (5) There are too many carbohydrates in this diet for good health.

<u>Questions 3 and 4</u> refer to the following information.

Weather balloons and airships such as blimps rise through the air because they are filled with a gas that is less dense than air. These gases are usually either hydrogen or helium. Hydrogen is the least dense of all gases, but it is flammable and ignites easily. Several airships have been destroyed because the hydrogen they contained ignited and burned. Unlike hydrogen, helium is nonflammable. However, helium is twice as dense as hydrogen, so it has less lifting power than hydrogen.

Hot-air balloons are filled with air that is heated by a gas burner beneath the balloon. These balloons rise because hot air is less dense than cold air.

3. Which fact from the passage supports the conclusion that helium is safer than hydrogen for filling balloons and airships?

   (1) Hydrogen is the least dense of all gases.
   (2) Helium is nonflammable.
   (3) Helium is twice as dense as hydrogen.
   (4) Helium has less lifting power than hydrogen.
   (5) Hot air is less dense than cold air.

4. A balloon filled with carbon dioxide will sink in hot air. What can you conclude about carbon dioxide?

   (1) It is flammable.
   (2) It leaks out of the balloon.
   (3) It is not a gas.
   (4) It is less dense than hydrogen.
   (5) It is denser than hot air.

Questions 5 and 6 refer to the following information and graph.

Coal is a fossil fuel that is burned to produce energy. The more carbon a sample of coal contains, the more energy it produces. The graphs below show the composition of coals from two mines.

Composition of Coal from Two Mines

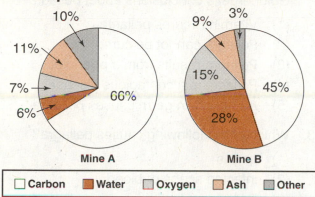

Mine A   Mine B

☐ Carbon ▩ Water ▨ Oxygen ▩ Ash ▩ Other

5. Which statement best summarizes information shown in these graphs?

   (1) Coals from both mines contain nitrogen.
   (2) Coals from both mines contain oxygen.
   (3) Coal from mine A contains more water.
   (4) Coal from mine B contains more ash.
   (5) Coal from mine B is harder and darker.

6. Which fact is needed to verify the conclusion that coal from mine A produces more energy than coal from mine B?

   (1) Coal from mine A contains more carbon.
   (2) Coal from mine A contains more "other" substances.
   (3) Coal from mine A contains less oxygen.
   (4) Coal from mine B burns more slowly.
   (5) Coal from mine B comes from deeper in the ground.

Question 7 refers to the following information.

Acids taste sour and turn litmus paper red. Acids include lemon juice, vinegar, and tomato juice. Bases taste bitter and turn litmus paper blue. Bases include toothpaste and milk of magnesia. The pH scale measures how acidic or basic a substance is. Acids have a pH less than 7, while bases have a pH greater than 7.

7. Unknown substance X has a pH of 5. Which conclusion about substance X can be verified?

   (1) It is lemon juice.
   (2) It is toothpaste.
   (3) It is a base.
   (4) It turns litmus paper red.
   (5) It tastes bitter.

Question 8 refers to the following information.

Sea level was not always the same as it is today. Ancient beaches on slopes above the Pacific Ocean show that these slopes were once at sea level. Wood was discovered on the ocean floor off the eastern coast of North America. Mineral formations that grow only above water have been found in undersea caves. These two findings show that such areas were once above sea level.

8. Which fact from the passage supports the conclusion that sea level was once higher?

   (1) Sea levels are ever changing.
   (2) Wood was discovered on the ocean floor.
   (3) There are ancient beaches on slopes above the ocean.
   (4) Mineral formations have been found in undersea caves.
   (5) Some areas under the ocean were once above sea level.

SCIENCE SKILLS PRACTICE 4

Check your answers on page 169.

Mini-Test • Unit 3

This is a 15-minute practice test. After 15 minutes, mark the last number you finished. Then complete the test and check your answers. If most of your answers were correct but you did not finish, try to work faster next time.

Directions: Choose the <u>one best answer</u> to each question.

<u>Questions 1 through 3</u> refer to the following information.

In the early 20th century, a disease called pellagra was sweeping the United States. People with the disease suffered itchy skin, diarrhea, dementia, and, for many, even death. In 1914, Joseph Goldberger, who was experienced at investigating epidemics, was asked to investigate pellagra. He observed that people living in prisons and other institutions got pellagra, but the staff did not. From this, he ruled out germs as the cause of the disease and turned toward diet. He tested his idea and found that a diet of fresh meat, milk, and vegetables cured pellagra and prevented it in healthy people. He later injected himself and others with the scabs and blood of people infected with pellagra. None of these people caught pellagra. Goldberger carried out experiment after experiment—all showing that diet and not germs caused pellagra—but many people did not believe his conclusions. Eight years after his death, it was shown that vitamin B cured pellagra. Goldberger had been right.

1. What question did Goldberger investigate?

    (1) What causes pellagra?
    (2) What is the healthiest diet?
    (3) What are the symptoms of pellagra?
    (4) What kinds of germs cause pellagra?
    (5) How come prison staffs do not get pellagra?

2. Which of the following best summarizes Goldberger's conclusions about pellagra?

    (1) Vitamin B cures pellagra.
    (2) Pellagra cannot be cured.
    (3) Pellagra results from a poor diet.
    (4) Pellagra is a contagious disease.
    (5) An unknown germ causes pellagra.

3. Which of the following causes pellagra?

    (1) germs
    (2) infected scabs or blood
    (3) living in an institution
    (4) a diet of meat and milk
    (5) a lack of vitamin B

<u>Question 4</u> refers to the following table.

Types of Storms

Storm	How long it lasts	Wind speed in miles/hour
Tornado	A few minutes	200–300
Hurricane	One week	74–200
Cyclone	More than a week	0–50

4. How are hurricanes and cyclones alike?

    They both

    (1) have very strong winds
    (2) last a week or longer
    (3) cause minimal damage
    (4) last only a few minutes
    (5) are more powerful than tornadoes

Questions 5 and 6 refer to the following diagram.

How an Air Bag Works

1. The crash sensor detects the crash.
2. The inflator starts a chemical reaction.
3. The chemical reaction makes nitrogen gas, which fills the air bag.

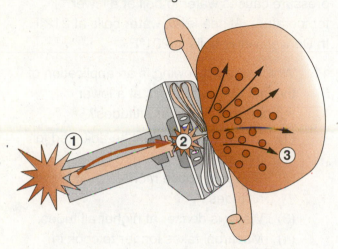

5. According to the diagram, which of the following happens last?

   (1) The crash detector triggers the chemical reaction.
   (2) The chemical reaction begins in the inflator.
   (3) The crash detector senses a crash.
   (4) The air bag inflates with nitrogen gas.
   (5) The chemical reaction produces nitrogen gas.

6. Which of the following is a direct effect of the nitrogen gas in the diagram?

   (1) The chemical reaction triggers a crash.
   (2) The air bag senses a crash.
   (3) The crash sensor triggers the inflator.
   (4) The chemical reaction begins.
   (5) The air bag inflates.

Questions 7 and 8 refer to the following information.

Most species have two names: a scientific name and a common name. Common names vary from place to place and from language to language. Unlike common names, scientific names are always the same.

Scientific names are in Latin, so scientists who speak all different languages can understand them. Scientific names are made up of two words. The first word tells the genus, or large group, to which the living thing belongs. The second word gives the species identifier within the genus.

7. How do scientific names and common names differ?

   (1) Scientific names are different in different languages.
   (2) Common names are always in Latin.
   (3) Scientific names are randomly assigned to species.
   (4) Common names are different in different languages.
   (5) Common names tells what genus the living thing belongs to.

8. Which of the following best restates the information from the second paragraph?

   (1) Species are named by both a scientific name and a common name.
   (2) Only the second word in a scientific name is important.
   (3) Scientific names vary from place to place and from language to language.
   (4) Since scientific names are in Latin, scientists must learn to read and write in Latin as well as in their own language.
   (5) Scientific names are made up of two Latin words, which tell the genus and the species of an organism.

Questions 9 and 10 refer to the following information and graph.

Tornadoes are produced by severe thunderstorms. The graph below shows the average number of tornadoes by month in the United States from 1950 through 1999.

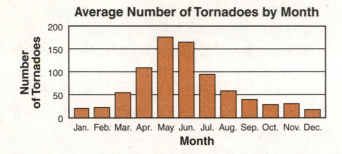

Average Number of Tornadoes by Month

9. Which statement summarizes information in the graph?

    (1) March and April have the greatest number of tornadoes.
    (2) More tornadoes occur in February than in August.
    (3) The number of tornadoes rises from January through May.
    (4) The number of tornadoes rises from July through December.
    (5) The number of tornadoes is about the same each month.

10. What can you conclude from the graph?

    (1) There is no chance that a tornado will occur in the winter.
    (2) Tornadoes are most likely to occur in May and June.
    (3) Tornadoes cause more damage in the fall than in the spring.
    (4) Tornadoes did not occur in the United States before 1950.
    (5) Tornadoes do not occur outside the United States.

Question 11 refers to the following information.

Air pressure decreases with altitude. At sea level, normal air pressure equals 14.7 pounds per square inch (psi). In Denver, Colorado, which is 1 mile above sea level, the air pressure is only about 12 psi. The decrease in air pressure causes water to boil at a lower temperature. At sea level, water boils at 212°F. In Denver, water boils at 201°F.

11. Which of the following is an application of the fact that water boils at a lower temperature at higher altitudes?

    (1) Thermometers must be adjusted for altitude.
    (2) Stoves produce more heat at higher altitudes.
    (3) Water is denser at higher altitudes.
    (4) Macaroni takes longer to cook in Denver.
    (5) Water is colder at high altitudes.

Question 12 refers to the following information.

Many buildings are made out of granite. Granite is a rock composed mainly of the minerals feldspar and quartz. It is usually white or gray with dark speckles. Granite is stronger than other rocks used for building, such as limestone and marble. It is also very resistant to weathering. Granite forms when molten rock cools very slowly beneath Earth's surface.

12. Which fact about granite supports the conclusion that it is useful for making monuments?

    (1) It is composed mainly of feldspar and quartz.
    (2) It is very resistant to weathering.
    (3) It is usually white or gray.
    (4) It forms beneath Earth's surface.
    (5) It forms when molten rock cools.

Questions 13 and 14 refer to the following information and graph.

The graphs below show the kinds of trees in two patches of a forest. One patch burned 25 years ago. The other burned 250 years ago.

Composition of Forest Patches After Fire

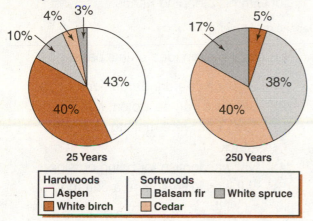

25 Years   250 Years

Hardwoods	Softwoods
☐ Aspen	▨ Balsam fir ▨ White spruce
■ White birch	▨ Cedar

13. Which of the following restates a fact presented in the graph?

   (1) There are more cedars after 250 years than 25 years.

   (2) There are more balsam firs than white birches after 25 years.

   (3) Aspens are present after 25 years and 250 years.

   (4) There are more softwoods than hardwoods after 25 years.

   (5) There are more hardwoods than softwoods after 250 years.

14. What can you conclude from the graphs?

   (1) Softwoods are more resistant to fire than hardwoods.

   (2) Softwoods are more resistant to insect damage than hardwoods.

   (3) Balsam fir and cedar grow faster than aspen and white birch.

   (4) The first trees to grow back after a fire are hardwoods.

   (5) The composition of a patch of forest remains the same after a fire.

Question 15 refers to the following information.

Smoke detectors provide an early warning of fire in a building. They work in various ways. Some use charged air molecules to create a small electric current inside the detector. When smoke particles bind to the air molecules, the current changes and an alarm sounds. Other smoke detectors use beams of light. An alarm sounds when smoke blocks or deflects the light.

15. What is another application of the principle behind smoke detectors that use light beams?

   (1) a touch-sensitive computer screen

   (2) a scale at a supermarket checkout counter

   (3) an automatic door activated by an electric eye

   (4) a burglar alarm activated by noise

   (5) a cooling fan turned on by high temperature

Question 16 refers to the following information.

In March 2000, 16 whales died when they became stranded on beaches in the Bahamas. The strandings occurred while the U.S. Navy was producing loud underwater sounds in the area. Scientists hypothesized that the whales stranded themselves because their ears were injured by the sounds. The scientists examined the heads of six of the dead whales. All six had injuries in or around their ears that could have been caused by loud sounds.

16. How did the scientists test their hypothesis?

   (1) They put the whales on beaches.

   (2) They produced loud underwater sounds.

   (3) They injured the ears of the whales.

   (4) They asked the U.S. Navy.

   (5) They examined six dead whales.

Check your answers on pages 169–170.

This posttest will help you see how well you have mastered GED critical thinking skills. Answer the questions below and check your answers on pages 170–174. Then use the Posttest Evaluation Chart on page 148 to evaluate your progress.

Directions: Choose the one best answer to each question.

Unit 1: Reading

Questions 1 through 4 refer to the following excerpt from a novel.

WHY ARE THE BIRDS ATTACKING?

Nat hurried on. Past the little wood, past the old barn, and then across the stile to the remaining field.

(5) As he jumped the stile he heard the whirr of wings. A black-backed gull dived down at him from the sky, missed, swerved in flight, and rose to dive again. In a moment it was joined by others, six, seven, a dozen, black-backed and herring
(10) mixed. Nat dropped his hoe. The hoe was useless. Covering his head with his arms he ran towards the cottage. They kept coming at him from the air, silent save for the beating wings. The terrible, fluttering
(15) wings. He could feel the blood on his hands, his wrists, his neck. Each stab of a swooping beak tore his flesh. If only he could keep them from his eyes. Nothing else mattered. He must keep them from
(20) his eyes. They had not learnt yet how to cling to a shoulder, how to rip clothing, how to dive in mass upon the head, upon the body. But with each dive, with each attack, they became bolder. And they had
(25) not thought for themselves. When they dived low and missed, they crashed, bruised and broken, on the ground. As Nat ran he stumbled, kicking their spent bodies in front of him.

(30) He found the door, he hammered upon it with his bleeding hands.

Daphne duMaurier, "The Birds"

1. What is the main idea of this passage?

   (1) Birds can be dangerous creatures.
   (2) Seagulls can be violent if provoked.
   (3) The birds were making an insane attack.
   (4) Nat was foolish for being outside.
   (5) Nat was lucky to find a cottage.

2. What can you infer from the sentence, "The hoe was useless" (lines 10–11)?

   (1) There were a lot of birds.
   (2) A hoe is an effective weapon.
   (3) Nat was too weak to fight.
   (4) The hoe was broken.
   (5) Birds like tools like hoes.

3. What does the author include the phrase, "They had not learnt yet how to cling to a shoulder, how to rip clothing" (Lines 20–21)?

   (1) to show that the birds could not learn
   (2) to show that the birds were enraged
   (3) to show that the attack was not serious
   (4) to show that Nat was not too afraid
   (5) to show that the attacks will worsen

4. Based on his behavior in this passage, what would Nat most likely do if he had an accident and cut himself?

   (1) He would become frantic and shout.
   (2) He would run wildly while bleeding.
   (3) He would wrap his wound and get help.
   (4) He would become confused and dizzy.
   (5) He would say that he had no problem.

Questions 5 through 8 refer to the following employee handbook.

WHAT IS IT LIKE TO WORK FOR THE UNIVERSITY DINING SERVICES?

Welcome to Cannon University Dining Services! We have been providing jobs for generations of Cannon students. In fact, we are the largest student employer (5) on campus.

As an employee of Cannon University Dining Services, you will gain valuable customer service experience. In addition, we hope that as part of our team you will (10) meet new friends and add to the quality of life at Cannon. This handbook contains guidelines on some key topics related to your employment.

Dining Services is first and foremost a (15) customer service organization. We want to provide the best service to the entire university community (students, faculty, staff, and guests). Therefore, all employees are expected to conduct (20) themselves in a professional manner. We encourage our employees to take responsibility and anticipate needs on the job. This is what has allowed us to provide high-quality customer service year after (25) year.

For health and safety, all workers must wear long pants, tee shirts (not tank tops) and closed-toe shoes. Large jewelry, shorts, short skirts, and torn clothing are (30) prohibited. Employees must wash their hands before work, when returning to work, after using the restroom, and after contaminating their hands in any other way.

5. Which of the following details supports the idea that Dining Services emphasizes customer service?

   (1) Cannon has hired generations of students.
   (2) Employees make new friends.
   (3) Workers must wear long pants.
   (4) Cannon employs a large number of students.
   (5) Cannon wants to provide the best service to the university community.

6. What is the effect of the first two paragraphs?

   It makes the working conditions sound

   (1) important and serious
   (2) low-paying and boring
   (3) difficult but fun
   (4) friendly and casual
   (5) overwhelming but worthwhile

7. If Cannon University also ran an art museum, which of the following could be expected?

   (1) It would not be open to the public.
   (2) It would expect visitors to be responsible.
   (3) Students would work there.
   (4) There would be reminders about safety.
   (5) The workers would not dress casually.

8. What conclusion about Cannon University Dining Services can you draw from the handbook?

   (1) The business is a failure.
   (2) Students get excellent work experience.
   (3) Workers want to dress formally.
   (4) Students learn to cook.
   (5) The food is very good.

Go on to the next page.

Questions 9 through 12 refer to the following excerpt from a novel.

WHAT IS NICK DOING?

Nick dropped his pack and rod-case and looked for a level piece of ground. He was very hungry and he wanted to make his camp before he cooked. Between two
(5) jack pines, the ground was quite level. He took the ax out of the pack and chopped out two projecting roots. That leveled a piece of ground large enough to sleep on. He smoothed out the sandy soil with his
(10) hand and pulled all the sweet fern bushes by their roots. His hands smelled good from the sweet fern. He smoothed the up-rooted earth. He did not want anything making lumps under the blankets. When
(15) he had the ground smooth, he spread his three blankets. One he folded double, next to the ground. The other two he spread on top.

With the ax he slit off a bright slab of
(20) pine from one of the stumps and split it into pegs for the tent. He wanted them long and solid to hold in the ground. With the tent unpacked and spread on the ground, the pack, leaning against a
(25) jackpine, looked much smaller. Nick tied the rope that served the tent for a ridge-pole to the trunk of one of the pine trees and pulled the tent up off the ground with the other end of the rope and tied it to the
(30) other pine. The tent hung on the rope like a canvas blanket on a clothesline. Nick poked a pole he had cut up under the back peak of the canvas and then made it a tent by pegging out the sides.

Ernest Hemingway, "Big Two-Hearted River: Part I"

9. What can be inferred about the man in this passage?

   (1) He is being chased.
   (2) He is poor.
   (3) He prefers to be outdoors.
   (4) He is in the mountains.
   (5) He has camped before.

10. When did Nick make his bed?

   (1) after he put up his tent
   (2) before he put up his tent
   (3) while he was smoothing the ground
   (4) after he had something to eat
   (5) while it was getting dark

11. Based on the information in this passage, which of the following best describes Nick?

   (1) clean and neat
   (2) orderly and organized
   (3) kind and compassionate
   (4) creative and artistic
   (5) picky and rude

12. Hemingway often writes about heroes who are both tough and tender.

   Based on this, and the information in the excerpt, which of the following best describes the tender side of Nick?

   (1) He wanted to make camp before cooking a meal.
   (2) He leveled a large piece of ground to sleep on.
   (3) He carefully made his bed, smoothing out any lumps.
   (4) He used the ax to cut off a slab of pine.
   (5) He tied the tent with rope, between two trees.

Questions 13 through 16 refer to the following excerpt from a review.

DOES THE REVIEWER LIKE THIS BOOK?

"Dirt Music," by Australian novelist Tim Winton, is that kind of novel—as rich, deep and delicious as a Godiva truffle and every bit as irresistible.

(5) You're tempted to linger over the language, relishing each sparkling sentence. But the characters are too compelling, the plot too intriguing. You simply have to race to the end to find out
(10) who does what, and how, and why.

Then, your curiosity satisfied, your emotions calmed, you can settle down for that second slow reading.

At its heart, "Dirt Music" is a story
(15) about love and music and the allure of each. It is also a classic love triangle, with each protagonist haunted by the past, terrified of the future but compelled by forces beyond her control to take action.

(20) Georgie Jutland, a jaded free spirit, has ended up in a remote fishing town in southwestern Australia. She is living with Jim Buckridge, a prosperous fisherman with a mysterious menacing past.

(25) But she is drawn to Luther Fox, a musician who has turned his back on music for the painful memories it evokes.

Between the two men is a legacy of distrust and antipathy, which Georgie's
(30) conflicted loyalties cause to flare dangerously.

Is it possible to make amends for the past? Can people change their essential nature through force of will? Can music
(35) be silenced, feelings be stifled? Or must music be heard, feelings be felt?

Winton explores these questions as his tangled tale unravels amid the wild isolation of western Australia's deserts and coastal islands.

"Aussie novelist makes beautiful 'Music'"
Jean Patteson

13. What is the main point of the first three paragraphs?

 (1) This novel is good to read while having a rich meal.
 (2) This novel is too rich, like too much chocolate.
 (3) This novel is so engaging that you may need to read it twice.
 (4) This novel isn't as good as an irresistible dessert.
 (5) This novel is very sappy and overly sweet.

14. How are Jim and Luther alike?

 (1) They are both wealthy.
 (2) They are both distrustful of Georgie.
 (3) They are both musicians.
 (4) They are both interested in Georgie.
 (5) They are both fishermen.

15. Based on the review, what type of art would this reviewer probably enjoy?

The reviewer would enjoy art that is

 (1) models and abstract
 (2) clear and literal
 (3) thought-provoking and intellectual
 (4) romantic and powerful
 (5) classic and depressing

16. What is the tone of this review?

 (1) disappointed
 (2) enthusiastic
 (3) tranquil
 (4) sarcastic
 (5) ominous

Go on to the next page. **139**

Unit 2: Social Studies

Questions 17 and 18 refer to the following information.

In feudal Japan (A.D. 1185–1871) the samurai were powerful warriors. During the early years of this era, however, the wives of samurai had a position that was similar to that of their husbands. For example, samurai wives trained to use weapons. They needed this skill to protect their households from enemy attack in their husbands' absence. Some samurai wives fought beside their husbands on the battlefield, too. Husbands and wives alike were expected to live by a code of honor. They even shared the traditional responsibility of committing suicide if they brought dishonor upon their families.

17. Which statement best summarizes this passage?

    (1) In samurai families, women as well as men could go to battle.
    (2) In the early feudal period, samurai men and their wives had some equality.
    (3) The samurai were warriors of ancient Japan.
    (4) During its feudal period, Japan was ruled by the samurai.
    (5) Samurai wives were expected to kill themselves when their husbands died.

18. What was the effect of giving samurai wives weapons training?

    (1) better-defended samurai property
    (2) a rise in Japan's suicide rate
    (3) an army of warrior women
    (4) demands for full equality with men
    (5) larger armies in battle

Questions 19 and 20 refer to the following photograph.

19. What is the MOST LIKELY reason for building this house on stilts?

    The design, an adaptation to life in that place, helps protects the house from

    (1) drought
    (2) insects
    (3) cold winds
    (4) flooding
    (5) lava flows

20. The planning that went into this building is the same kind of thinking that goes into which of the following?

    (1) installing energy-efficient appliances in new homes
    (2) including tornado-safe rooms in new homes
    (3) adding wheelchair ramps to public buildings
    (4) building high-rise apartments in large, crowded cities
    (5) putting fences around swimming pools

Questions 21 and 22 refer to the following information.

In October 1957, the Soviet Union launched *Sputnik I,* the world's first artificial satellite. The American public, already filled with Cold War anxiety, felt threatened. After all, they reasoned, if the Soviets could launch satellites into orbit, they might be able to launch nuclear missiles against the United States. American scientists, who themselves were working on a satellite, were surprised and embarrassed. Americans were determined to prove their scientific superiority, and the "Space Race" began. For the next dozen years, the two nations competed for "firsts" in space—the first human to orbit the earth, then the first space walk, then the first unmanned lunar mission, and so on—until the *Apollo XI* mission put Americans on the moon in July 1969.

21. Which statement expresses a belief that lead to U.S. involvement in the "Space Race"?

(1) Americans are explorers by nature and must explore space.
(2) The Soviet Union is the enemy of all democratic people.
(3) Only the United States can protect the world.
(4) Only the United States can end the Cold War.
(5) The United States is better than other countries.

22. Which event took place first?

(1) the launch of *Sputnik I*
(2) the first unmanned lunar mission
(3) the start of the Cold War
(4) the flight of the first astronaut
(5) the American landing on the moon

Questions 23 and 24 refer to the following line graph.

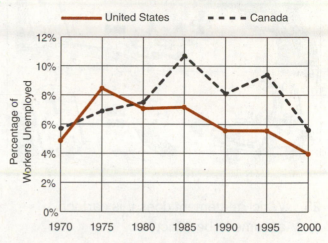

Unemployment Rates in the United States and Canada, 1970–2000

Source: Bureau of Labor Statistics, U.S. Department of Labor

23. Which statement best summarizes the information on this graph?

(1) Historically, unemployment is a bigger problem in the United States than in Canada.
(2) Unemployment is higher in North America than anywhere else.
(3) About 8% of workers in these countries are out of work at any given time.
(4) During this period, employment varied more in Canada than in the United States.
(5) In both countries, too many people are out of work.

24. In which year was the unemployment rate in the United States higher than the unemployment rate in Canada?

(1) 1970
(2) 1975
(3) 1980
(4) 1990
(5) 2000

Go on to the next page.

Questions 25 and 26 refer to the following political cartoon.

25. Which statement does this cartoon assume to be a fact?

    (1) People have died in accidents caused by drivers using cell phones.
    (2) If more people used cell phones, help for accident victims would arrive faster.
    (3) Criminals who use guns should receive harsh punishments.
    (4) Americans need stricter gun control.
    (5) Cell phones should be outlawed.

26. Which of the following statements best reflects a belief of the cartoonist?

    (1) No matter what the cause, everyone eventually dies.
    (2) Guns should be outlawed.
    (3) Using a cell phone while driving is as dangerous as a loaded gun.
    (4) Cell phones cause more deaths than guns.
    (5) Neither guns nor cell phones can hurt people if they are used responsibly.

Questions 27 and 28 refer to the following quotation from the 1954 Supreme Court decision in *Brown* v. *Board of Education.*

In these days, it is doubtful that any child may reasonably be expected to succeed in life if he is denied the opportunity of an education. Such an opportunity, where the state has undertaken to provide it, is a right which must be made available to all on equal terms.

We come then to the question presented: Does segregation of children in public schools solely on the basis of race, even though the physical facilities and other "tangible" factors may be equal, deprive the children of the minority group of equal educational opportunities? We believe that it does.

27. Which of the following best restates the first sentence of this quotation?

    (1) Racial segregation denies all that the United States represents.
    (2) An uneducated child will probably achieve little as an adult.
    (3) Educating children is our nation's highest priority.
    (4) Every state has the responsibility to educate its children.
    (5) Most children do not understand the value of their education.

28. People who agree with the second paragraph would be most likely to support which of the following?

    (1) better facilities in minority schools
    (2) military academies
    (3) "separate but equal" schools
    (4) tuition-free college education
    (5) multicultural education in schools

Questions 29 and 30 refer to the following map.

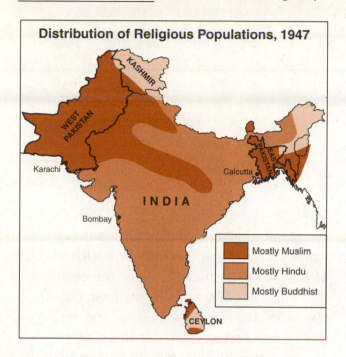

Distribution of Religious Populations, 1947

Legend:
- Mostly Muslim
- Mostly Hindu
- Mostly Buddhist

29. According to this map, what did West Pakistan and East Pakistan have in common in 1947?

   (1) a large number of mountain ranges
   (2) vast stretches of desert
   (3) a largely Buddhist population
   (4) a largely Muslim population
   (5) a largely Hindu population

30. Which behavior would you predict was the most logical outcome of the creation of West Pakistan?

   (1) violence erupting between Buddhists and Muslims
   (2) Hindus fleeing to West Pakistan
   (3) Hindus fleeing to India
   (4) Hindus demanding Kashmir as an independent homeland
   (5) Muslims demanding control of Ceylon

Questions 31 and 32 refer to the following information.

     Leasing cars has become popular, but is leasing the right choice for you? If you will use the car for five years or longer, you probably should pay off a car loan instead of continuing to pay on a lease. Likewise, if you will drive more than 15,000 miles a year, leasing could become very expensive. On the other hand, a lease lets you drive a more expensive car for the same monthly payment as buying a less expensive car. In addition, replacing one new car with another every two or three years may be more important to you than the money involved. Just think carefully about your preferences and your use of the car before you decide.

31. Which of the following statements is an opinion rather than a fact?

   (1) It is foolish to lease a car instead of buying one.
   (2) You often will pay less for a used car than for a new one.
   (3) Putting a lot of mileage onto a leased car makes leasing more expensive.
   (4) Leasing is an option for potential new car owners.
   (5) When you lease a car, it does not belong to you.

32. For which statement does the passage provide factual support?

   (1) People who lease a car usually wish that they had bought it instead.
   (2) Buying a car is often more economical than leasing one.
   (3) More people lease cars than buy them.
   (4) More people buy cars than lease them.
   (5) Few people drive their cars more than 15,000 miles in a year.

Go on to the next page.

Unit 3: Science

Questions 33 and 34 refer to the following information and graph.

The characteristics of soils depend on their composition. Soils that contain a lot of sand have many pore spaces, so they get a lot of air. The pores allow these soils to drain rapidly, so sandy soils do not hold much water. Soils that contain a lot of clay can hold a large amount of water. That makes these soils gummy and slippery when they are wet. When they are dry, clay-rich soils are very hard. The graphs below show the composition of two soils.

Composition of Two Soils

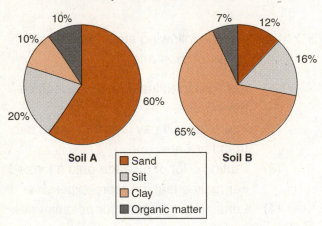

33. What information in the graphs supports the conclusion that soil A is well-aerated?

   (1) Soil A exists in a very windy area.
   (2) Organic matter is found only in well-aerated soils.
   (3) Soil A consists of equal parts clay and organic matter.
   (4) Soil A has about as much silt as soil B.
   (5) The largest component of soil A is sand.

34. Which of the following would be a good use of soil B?

   (1) making bricks, tiles, and pottery
   (2) making an all-weather road
   (3) growing plants that need semi-dry soil
   (4) growing plants that need good aeration of their roots
   (5) providing drainage around a house's foundation

Question 35 refers to the following information.

Many coastal cities are built near estuaries. An estuary is a partly-enclosed body of water where a river flows into the ocean. San Francisco Bay and Chesapeake Bay are two examples of large estuaries. The mixing of fresh water and salt water in an estuary creates a good environment for many kinds of wildlife. Several types of fish and shellfish begin their lives in estuaries. Migrating birds rest and feed in estuaries. However, people have drained and filled in large areas of estuaries to make new land for buildings and farms. As a result, most estuaries are much smaller now than they once were.

35. Which fact in the passage supports the conclusion that estuaries are in danger?

   (1) An estuary is a partly enclosed body of water.
   (2) San Francisco Bay is an example of a large estuary.
   (3) Most estuaries are much smaller than they once were.
   (4) Fresh water and salt water mix in an estuary.
   (5) Many fish and shellfish begin their lives in estuaries.

Question 36 refers to the following information.

The Hawaiian Islands are a chain of volcanoes in the Pacific Ocean. The oldest volcano is in the northwest part of the chain. The youngest is in the southeast. These volcanoes all formed over a "hot spot" in the mantle—the layer of Earth below the crust. For millions of years, the crust beneath the Pacific Ocean has been moving very slowly to the northwest. As it moves over the hot spot, new volcanoes are formed.

36. What can you conclude about where the next volcano in the chain will form?

   (1) It will form in the north.
   (2) It will form in the northeast.
   (3) It will form in the northwest.
   (4) It will form in the southeast.
   (5) It will form in the southwest.

Question 37 refers to the following information.

The indigo bunting is a bird that breeds in the eastern United States and migrates south each fall. A scientist at Cornell University proposed that migrating buntings navigate by using the stars. He tested this idea by raising two groups of young buntings in a planetarium. One group saw the normal pattern of night stars. In the fall, these birds oriented themselves toward the south. The other group was shown an artificial night sky in which the position of the stars was shifted. The birds in this group oriented toward the direction of south in the artificial sky.

37. What hypothesis did the scientist test?

   (1) Buntings breed in the United States.
   (2) Buntings migrate south each fall.
   (3) Buntings navigate by using the stars.
   (4) Buntings can be raised in a planetarium.
   (5) Buntings orient toward the south.

Question 38 refers to the following information.

An earthquake produces seismic waves that travel away from the earthquake's epicenter. These waves are detected by seismic recording stations around the world. By measuring how long it takes the waves from an earthquake to reach each of three stations, scientists can locate the epicenter of the earthquake.

38. Which of the following is an application of the idea behind locating an earthquake's epicenter?

   (1) using three computers at the same time to perform calculations more quickly
   (2) using three listeners in different places to find a bird that can be heard but not seen
   (3) repeating an experiment three times to be more certain of the result
   (4) collecting water samples from three lakes to find out if any are polluted
   (5) measuring a plant's height over three weeks to see how quickly it grows

Question 39 refers to the following graph.

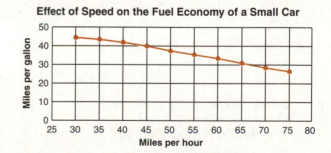

Effect of Speed on the Fuel Economy of a Small Car

39. What conclusion can be drawn from the graph?

   (1) Fuel economy is not related to speed.
   (2) A car uses less gas when driven fast.
   (3) Driving slowly is more economical.
   (4) Newer cars are more economical.
   (5) Large cars use more gas than small cars.

    Go on to the next page.

Questions 40 and 41 refer to the following information.

Wind can make it feel colder than it is. For example, a wind of 35 miles per hour can make 10°F feel like −35°F. This effect is called wind chill. Wind chill can be defined as the rate of heat lost from a person's skin due to wind and cold.

Wind Chill Temperatures

Wind speed (in miles per hour)

Temperatures (in °F)

Calm	20	15	10	5	0	−5	−10	−15	−20
5	13	7	1	−5	−11	−16	−22	−28	−34
10	9	3	−4	−10	−16	−22	−28	−35	−41
15	6	0	−7	−13	−19	−26	−32	−39	−45
20	4	−2	−9	−15	−22	−29	−35	−42	−48
25	3	−4	−11	−17	−24	−31	−37	−44	−51
30	1	−5	−12	−19	−26	−33	−39	−46	−53
35	0	−7	−14	−21	−27	−34	−41	−48	−55
40	−1	−8	−15	−22	−29	−36	−43	−50	−57
45	−2	−9	−16	−23	−30	−37	−44	−51	−58

☐ Frostbite can occur in 30 minutes or less.

40. What effect does a 30-mile-per-hour wind have on a temperature of 0°F?

The wind causes the temperature to feel like

(1)   26°F
(2)   −0°F
(3)   −19°F
(4)   −26°F
(5)   −30°F

41. What causes wind chill?

(1) falling temperatures
(2) calm winds
(3) wind and cold
(4) frostbite
(5) negative temperatures

Questions 42 and 43 refer to the following information.

The aspartame used to sweeten foods was discovered accidentally. A researcher working on anti-ulcer drugs traced a sweet taste on his finger to his workbench. He and his colleague then tried the substance in their morning coffee. Similarly, saccharine was discovered when a researcher noticed that his dinner tasted sweet. He found the sweet taste on his skin, and later in his lab. The sweeteners cyclamate and sucrolase were also discovered when researchers accidentally tasted them.

42. How was the discovery of aspartame similar to the discovery of saccharine?

(1) They were both discovered in coffee.
(2) They were both discovered after many years of testing chemicals for sweetness.
(3) They were both discovered at meals.
(4) They were both discovered when they were accidentally tasted.
(5) They were both discovered by the same team of researchers.

43. Which observations led to the discovery of aspartame?

(1) testing anti-ulcer drugs for sweetness
(2) testing different substances in coffee
(3) tasting a substance accidentally spilled on fingers
(4) finding a sweet taste at dinner one night
(5) many years of hunting for a sugar substitute

Questions 44 and 45 refer to the following information and diagram.

A refrigerant chemical moves through the coils of the air conditioner. When the chemical changes states, it moves the heat from the inside to the outside of the house.

How an Air Conditioner Works

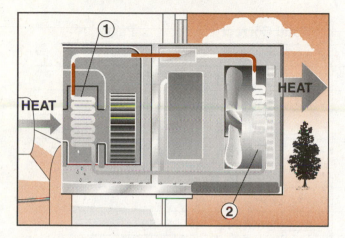

44. According to the diagram, which of the following happens first?

   (1) Heat is given off outside.
   (2) The air conditioner's fan blows heat from the room.
   (3) The air conditioner's fan pulls in heat from the room.
   (4) The coils in the air conditioner absorb the heat.
   (5) Gas in the air conditioner is blown into the room.

45. Which of the following best summarizes how an air conditioner works?

   (1) Heat inside the house is moved outside of the house.
   (2) The liquid in the air conditioner evaporates the heat inside the house.
   (3) The air conditioner blows the heated liquid out of the house.
   (4) The heat in the air conditioner moves into the house.
   (5) The gas in the air conditioner condenses the heat in the house.

Question 46 refers to the following information.

46. Two common pain relievers that are available over the counter are acetaminophen and ibuprofen. Both reduce fever and relieve pain. Ibuprofen reduces swelling and other symptoms of inflammation, but it also upsets the stomach. Too much acetaminophen can damage the liver.

According to the passage, which of the following is one way ibuprofen differs from acetaminophen?

Unlike acetaminophen, ibuprofen

   (1) reduces fever
   (2) relieves pain
   (3) can damage the liver
   (4) can cause swelling
   (5) reduces inflammation

Question 47 refers to the following information.

47. Rechargeable batteries are batteries that can be used again and again. When compared to other batteries, rechargeable batteries may seem expensive, but considering their long life, they are actually the most economical choice. Since they are reused, these batteries do not end up in landfills, and so are also better for the environment than regular batteries.

Which of the following restates the last sentence of the paragraph?

Rechargeable batteries

   (1) help to preserve the natural world
   (2) are more expensive than regular batteries
   (3) fill up landfills
   (4) are rarely reused
   (5) are economical for high-use devices

 Go on to the next page.

Posttest Evaluation Chart

After you have completed the Postttest, check your answers on pages 170–174. On the chart below circle the number of each question that you answered correctly on the Posttest. Count the number of questions you answered correctly in each row. Write the number in the total correct space in each row. (For example, in the Reading: Comprehension row, write the number correct in the blank before *out of 4*.) Complete this process for the remaining rows.

Content Area	Questions	Total Correct	Pages
Unit 1: Reading			
Comprehension	1, 2, 5, 13	_____ out of 4	14–19
Application	4, 7, 15	_____ out of 3	44–45
Analysis	6, 8, 9, 10, 11	_____ out of 5	22–27, 30–31, 36–39
Synthesis	3, 12, 14, 16	_____ out of 4	32–33, 40–41, 46–47
	TOTAL	_____ **out of 16**	
Unit 2: Social Studies			
Comprehension	17, **23,** 27	_____ out of 3	56–59
Application	**20,** 28	_____ out of 2	78–79
Analysis	18, **19,** 22, **24, 25, 29, 30,** 31	_____ out of 8	64–69, 76–77
Evaluation	21, **26,** 32	_____ out of 3	74–75, 84–87
	TOTAL	_____ **out of 16**	
Unit 3: Science			
Comprehension	43, **44, 45,** 47	_____ out of 4	98–101
Application	**34,** 38	_____ out of 2	118–119
Analysis	37, **39, 40, 41,** 42, 46	_____ out of 6	106–111, 116–117
Evaluation	**33,** 35, 36	_____ out of 3	124–127
	TOTAL	_____ **out of 15**	

Compare your Posttest scores with your Pretest scores on the Pretest Evaluation Chart on page 11. Talk with your teacher about how you can do more work on important preGED critical thinking skills.

Question numbers that are in **bold** are based on graphics.

PRETEST

UNIT 1: READING

PAGE 4

1. **(5) The children and wife are fearful of the father's temper.** *(Fiction: Comprehension)* All of the details and actions of the characters focus on the father's anger. For example, the author describes Lillian's desperate look to indicate her fear.

2. **(1) She wants to protect them from their father.** *(Fiction: Comprehension)* Lillian asks the children to be quiet, but only after her husband has yelled at them. She also gives them a desperate look, which shows her fear of what the father would do if they weren't quiet.

3. **(5) get upset with the waiter** *(Fiction: Application)* The point of the passage is that the father has a very nasty temper. Therefore, he would most likely get angry with the person who brought him the meal.

PAGE 5

4. **(4) The other job-sharer would work 22 hours.** *(Nonfiction: Analysis)* Job-sharing employees share the duties of one full-time position, or 40 hours a week. If one employee worked 18 hours, the other employee would have to work 22 hours.

5. **(2) Job-sharers and part-time employees have benefits and flexible hours.** *(Nonfiction: Analysis)* Job-sharers and part-time employees receive benefits, which include family leave, and have flexible hours. Therefore, employees would have more time to attend to family business.

6. **(4) business-like** *(Nonfiction: Synthesis)* The vocabulary and sentence structure are very straightforward.

UNIT 2: SOCIAL STUDIES

PAGE 6

7. **(3) its many Great Lakes shorelines** *(Geography: Comprehension)* Michigan touches four of the five Great Lakes and has more shoreline than Wisconsin.

8. **(2) Milwaukee, Chicago, Kalamazoo, and Ann Arbor** *(Geography: Analysis)* This route goes south to Milwaukee and Chicago, and then east through Kalamazoo and Ann Arbor to Detroit.

9. **(2) Jeannette Rankin took a strong stand on the causes that mattered to her.** *(Civics and Government: Comprehension)* The passage notes Rankin's involvement with the suffrage and pacifist movements and her willingness to take an unpopular stand in Congress.

10. **(1) She opposed war in general.** *(Civics and Government: Evaluation)* The quote states her opposition to war in principle, and the other details about her life support that view.

PAGE 7

11. **(4) countries that are well-off are ignoring problems of poverty and starvation in other parts of the world** *(World History: Evaluation)* One person is enjoying plentiful resources (representing developed countries) while the other person (representing underdeveloped countries) is starving.

12. **(5) Action Against Hunger** *(World History: Application)* The cartoon shows a person who is starving in a drought-stricken land. Action Against Hunger would be the most likely agency to address this problem.

PAGE 8

13. **(3) Building schools is a wise use of oil money.** *(Economics: Analysis)* The word

wise indicates an opinion. The other options restate facts from the passage.

14. **(5) The price of gasoline would rise.** *(Economics: Analysis)* An oil embargo would create a shortage of oil. If there is a shortage of a product, prices go up.

UNIT 3: SCIENCE

PAGE 9

15. **(3) One pond had no algae growing in it.** *(Life Science: Science as Inquiry: Evaluation)* The farmer hypothesized that one of the ponds contained very little nitrogen because he observed that it had no algae growing in it.

16. **(1) The dough rises.** *(Life Science: Scientific Skills and Understanding: Analysis)* The yeast produces carbon dioxide, which causes the dough to rise.

17. **(2) how light passes through an SLR camera** *(Physical Science: Science and Technology: Comprehension)* The text and the diagram are about this topic.

18. **(5) It passes through a translucent screen.** *(Physical Science: Science and Technology: Analysis)* The arrow pointing up from the mirror shows that light is reflected through a translucent screen.

PAGE 10

19. **(3) They looked for evidence of a huge asteroid or comet collision.** *(Life Science: Science as Inquiry: Analysis)* According to the passage, scientists began looking for evidence that a huge asteroid or comet collided with Earth.

20. **(1) A large crater was formed about 65 million years ago.** *(Life Science: Science as Inquiry: Evaluation)* The crater was formed at about the same time that dinosaurs became extinct. This supports the idea that the collision of an asteroid or comet with Earth caused dinosaurs to become extinct.

21. **(4) Gypsum is softer than feldspar.** *(Earth and Space Science: Unifying Concepts and Processes: Comprehension)* The length of each bar indicates the hardness of that mineral. Gypsum's bar is shorter than feldspar's.

22. **(2) diamond** *(Earth and Space Science: Science and Technology: Application)* Diamond has the longest bar, which means it is the hardest mineral. Harder minerals are more durable, or longer lasting.

UNIT 1: READING

LESSON 1

PAGE 15

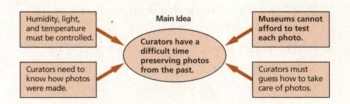

1. It is difficult to preserve photographs from the past.
2. **b**
3. **(2) Max worked very hard to be a good baseball player.** All of the details in the passage support this idea.

LESSON 2

PAGE 17

Who? Leo Stuart is a detective.	Supporting Details	What? He is digging in the ground.
When? He begins digging at sunrise.	Where? He is on a hillside.	Why or How? He is searching for something.

1. The second sentence says that he is "ten feet due east of the ancient bronze marker."
2. His shovel struck something hollow.

3. **(4) a soft-bodied animal that lives in a shell** The third sentence describes a mollusk.

LESSON 3

PAGE 19

Statement ⟶	Inference
• His owners begin every meal by giving him a scrap of food from their plates.	• His owners have trained him to beg by feeding him at the table.
• He will only stop if they shout, "Lie down!" Then Riley lies down on the floor immediately.	• **The owners use the command "Lie down" to discipline Riley.**
• His owners have tried reasoning with him, but nothing works.	• **The owners do not understand that you cannot reason with a dog.**

1. For each thing that Riley does wrong, the writer points out that the owners are also doing something wrong. The owners don't realize they are rewarding Riley's bad behavior. Clearly, Riley can be trained because he has learned to lie down on command.
2. **a**
3. **(3) in-home healthcare workers** Since all of the recommendations encourage changes that would benefit in-home healthcare workers, it would be reasonable to infer that the organization that conducted this study is one that works on their behalf.

READING PRACTICE 1

PAGE 20

1. **(4) Harmonicas are satisfying to play, portable, and cheap compared to guitars. (Comprehension: Main Idea)** The narrator discusses the joys of playing the harmonica, and contrasts this with the difficulties of playing the guitar. The other options address only a portion of the passage.
2. **(4) . . .in the tent door after supper. . . (Comprehension: Detail)** The narrator mentions playing the harmonica near the tent after supper. This tells something about where the narrator is located. The other options tell about the harmonica, but not about the setting.
3. **(1) content and thoughtful (Comprehension: Inference)** The narrator shares his thoughts about the harmonica and its positive attributes. The narrator is pleased with all the things the harmonica does.

PAGE 21

4. **(1) Be prepared for emergencies with your pet. (Comprehension: Main Idea)** The title is a strong clue to the main idea of this passage. The other options address only one part of the passage.
5. **(4) The vet may be closed when your pet is hurt. (Comprehension: Detail)** If your pet is hurt and your vet's office is closed, knowing where you can get help is critical.
6. **(2) to show it to people if your pet is lost (Comprehension: Inference)** If your pet is lost, it's important to be able to show people what it looks like so it can be found. There is no information in the passage to support the other options.
7. **(5) The kit must be easy to carry and locate and should have important items for a pet emergency. (Comprehension: Main Idea)** This best summarizes the point of this section. The other options include details that are important but are not the main idea.

LESSON 4

PAGE 23

Order of Events

1	Andrew wandered to the boathouse.
2	**He entered the building.**
3	**He struck a match and saw the lantern.**
4	He lit the lantern.
5	**He heard a voice behind him.**

1. Andrew had intended to walk to the farmhouse. However, he was so lost in thought that he ended up walking to the boathouse instead.
2. He struck a match from his pocket. He needed a light so he could see in the dark.
3. **(2) She placed the toy under the second cup.** The clapping is the distraction. Before she clapped, the doctor moved the toy and placed it under the second cup.

LESSON 5

PAGE 25

First U.S. Flags / Current U.S. Flag

First U.S. Flags	Red, white, and blue	Current U.S. Flag
No uniform design	White stars in a blue field	Uniform design
Stars had 4–8 points	13 alternating red & white stripes	50 five-pointed stars
Flags had additional symbols, colors, and pictures		13 horizontal red and white stripes

1. The current flag has fifty stars instead of thirteen.
2. b
3. **(4) Detroit and Sanibel** The paragraph describes some of the differences between Detroit and Sanibel.

LESSON 6

PAGE 27

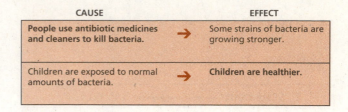

CAUSE		EFFECT
People use antibiotic medicines and cleaners to kill bacteria.	→	Some strains of bacteria are growing stronger.
Children are exposed to normal amounts of bacteria.	→	Children are healthier.

1. They hope to kill germs so they won't get sick.
2. The overuse of antibiotics and antibiotic cleaners causes more powerful strains of bacteria to flourish.
3. **(3) a smart marketing promotion and hard work** The marketing idea combined with hard work on the part of the workers in shipping and receiving resulted in a 5% increase over the last year's sales.

READING PRACTICE 2

PAGE 28

1. **(5) The romance helps the movie.** *(Comprehension: Main Idea)* The final paragraph focuses on the impact of the romance in this movie. The reviewer explains that it is rather lightweight, but the charisma and beauty of the two actors make it appealing.
2. **(5) Anakin and Obi-Wan are in both films.** *(Analysis: Compare and Contrast)* Based on the excerpt, the only correct response is that these characters are in both films.
3. **(2) Anakin can be frustrated by Obi-Wan** *(Analysis: Cause and Effect)* Reviewers often use quotes to emphasize a point. This quote shows how Anakin expresses his rebellion against his father figure.

PAGE 29

4. **(5) He had intended to go to Taulkinham.** *(Comprehension: Inference)* The excerpt says he waited until "the right train came,"

and "When he got to Taulkinham." Although the character appears to be directionless, we learn that he has a destination.

5. **(2) He saw signs and lights blinking frantically. *(Comprehension: Detail)*** The many signs and flashing lights are indications of a big city.

6. **(5) He appeared as if he had a purpose. *(Comprehension: Inference)*** This man, though perhaps an unhappy loner, is good at appearing like everyone else—as if he has a purpose.

7. **(5) He was not looking. *(Analysis: Cause and Effect)*** The passage states he was looking the other way when the train "slid off" and left the station.

8. **(5) He waited six hours. *(Analysis: Sequence)*** According to the passage, "He had to wait six hours at the junction stop until the right train came."

LESSON 7

Page 31

CONCLUSION				
Alan's fear is unreasonable.				
Alan is hugging the cliff wall.	F A C T S	The trail is paved and marked.	F A C T S	His family members are not scared; they are laughing and talking.

1. They are laughing and talking.
2. They do not take his fears seriously. They tease him and talk and laugh together, indicating that the situation is not dangerous.
3. **(3) Chavez's personal leadership played a strong role in the union's success.** This is the only conclusion that can be drawn based on the passage. Chavez founded the union, led it in launching a strike and a boycott, and fasted to bring the farm workers' plight to national attention.

LESSON 8

Page 33

Author's Purpose The author wants to persuade employees to help the company by complying with the new requests.	
Supporting Facts and Opinions The company must save money to avoid layoffs. Too many absences hurt productivity. Employees can help by giving one month's notice of vacation leave and scheduling planned absences.	Key Words and Phrases difficult time suffered substantial losses hurt our productivity, stretch our budget, your cooperation is critical, severe

1. The author is asking employees to help the company avoid budget cuts and layoffs by complying with the new requests.
2. The author uses words and phrases such as "suffered substantial losses," "difficult time," "stretch our budget," "your cooperation is critical," and "severe" to appeal to the readers' emotions.
3. **(5) gently** The repeated word "gently" suggests that the teacher is sensitive to the children's feelings.

READING PRACTICE 3

Page 34

1. **(4) He isn't sure it's right to shoot the man. *(Comprehension: Inference)*** Legolas isn't sure it's right to shoot an old man that looks so harmless. There is no evidence to support the other options.

2. **(1) appears harmless *(Analysis: Conclusion)*** This option is correct because Aragorn tells the group, "We may not shoot an old man so, at unawares and unchallenged, whatever fear or doubt be on us. Watch and wait!" The man is also described as old and feeble, which adds to the wisdom of Aragorn's decision.

3. **(2) He would rather be safe than sorry. *(Analysis: Character)*** Gimli insists on shooting and is impatient with Legolas for holding back. Gimli asks him what he is waiting for and why he doesn't shoot.

4. **(1) to make it seem like the man couldn't be harmful** *(Synthesis: Author's Purpose)* The author includes this detail to add more doubt that this person could be harmful; he appears too old and feeble. Some of the other options may be true, but they do not add to the main point— should this man be shot or not, and why?

PAGE 35

5. **(5) The reader should get rid of any pre-conceived ideas and be open to what the author has to give.** *(Comprehension: Main Idea)* The author states, "If you hang back, and reserve and criticise at first, you are preventing yourself from getting the fullest possible value from what you read." The author also states that there are separate classes of books, but really emphasizes that we should not bring preconceived ideas to each class.

6. **(1) It allows the reader to learn more from the author.** *(Analysis: Conclusion)* The purpose of this excerpt is to convince readers to keep an open mind to see what an author has to offer. This is supported in the passage by the phrases "open your mind," "the twist and turn of the first sentences will bring you into the presence of a human being unlike any other," and "you will find that your author is giving you. . . something far more definite." Each of these statements points to the reader learning from the author.

7. **(5) Join with the author's vision as you read.** *(Synthesis: Author's Purpose)* The author uses this statement to tell the reader to work along with the author and join the author in the journey of the book.

LESSON 9

PAGE 37

1. The author said that the astronauts were the scientists' "lab rats."
2. **a**
3. **(2) during the daytime** The best clue is that people who do road work generally work in the daytime.

LESSON 10

PAGE 39

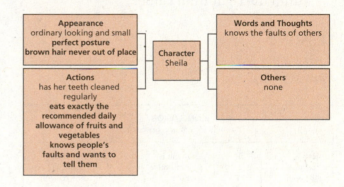

1. She cannot control her desire to tell people their flaws.
2. **b**
3. **(3) disapproving** Elio clearly doesn't like technology, but the facts do not support such strong feelings as fear or disgust.

LESSON 11

Who is present?	Abraham Lincoln, his opponent, a narrator
What is seen?	Lincoln's appearance
What is heard?	Part of the debate, comments about how Lincoln would look on television

+

| Point of view? | an outside narrator |

1. **b**
2. He would have described Lincoln as someone who is deceitful or hypocritical.
3. **(4) the mother's thoughts and feelings** The passage is written from the point of view of Warren's mother. The reader sees Warren and the passersby through her eyes.

READING PRACTICE 4

1. **(1) sad (Analysis: Tone)** The son realizes that his father is a bit out-of-touch and "isn't 'King Kong' Charlie Keller," the famous Yankee baseball player. This ends the passage on a sad note.
2. **(2) He feels distressed and decides to let it go. (Analysis: Character)** The son notices the father's misplaced grasp and states, "I am suddenly overcome with sadness."
3. **(2) enthusiastic (Analysis: Character)** The father is eager to play ball even though he is older and not holding the bat correctly.
4. **(2) ...the little boy upon whose head no rain shall ever fall (Synthesis: Point of View)** This option captures the father's view of his son. The other quotes are from the son's viewpoint.
5. **(1) ...back of my school. (Comprehension: Setting)** This option best describes where they are—on a dirt field, behind the son's school.

6. **(3) complex and interesting (Synthesis: Point of View)** The reviewer thought the filmmakers made intelligent choices and that the movie was charming and witty. He also mentions that the story line includes romance as well as crime fighting and that it had some dark aspects. This supports the idea that he thinks this movie is complex and interesting.
7. **(2) like the comic book in some ways (Comprehension: Inference)** the phrase "the most appealing parts" implies that the less appealing parts were not included in the movie; therefore the movie is like the comic only in some ways, not in all.
8. **(2) a spider bite (Analysis: Cause and Effect)** Peter was bitten by a spider, and the next day he woke up with superpowers. The connection between the two events is clear. Radiation was the cause of Peter's superpowers in the comic book, but not in the movie.

LESSON 12

New Situation	Given Information
Walter	Company Policy
OK	1. 40-hour work week
OK	2. no increased costs
OK	3. office covered
Sue	Company Policy
OK	1. 40-hour work week
OK	2. no increased costs
NO	3. office covered

1. Yes. This is within the scope of the new policies because Walter can do his job full-time, with no increased costs or problems for his department.
2. No. If Sue changed her schedule, she would not be available to discuss benefits issues with workers up to 5 P.M. That would violate the rule of keeping each office open during normal business hours.

3. **(1) No, it is not designed for hockey.** There are special dangers unique to each sport. A ski helmet does not protect against the special dangers related to hockey.

LESSON 13

PAGE 47

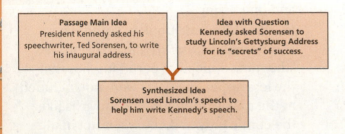

Passage Main Idea
President Kennedy asked his speechwriter, Ted Sorensen, to write his inaugural address.

Idea with Question
Kennedy asked Sorensen to study Lincoln's Gettysburg Address for its "secrets" of success.

Synthesized Idea
Sorensen used Lincoln's speech to help him write Kennedy's speech.

1. Kennedy knew that Lincoln's speech had been successful and wanted Sorensen to find out what had made it so successful.
2. Sorensen used the style of Lincoln's speech as the basis for writing Kennedy's speech.
3. **(2) determined** Based on the passage alone, any of the words could describe Russ. However, when you add the fact that the author bragged about his own trip across country, you see that he admires Russ and would see him as determined to keep going.

READING PRACTICE 5

PAGE 48

1. **(3) humorous (*Synthesis: Tone*)** This option is supported by the word choice and use of exaggeration throughout the review, such as "Ronnie is a jack-of-all-crimes," and "he knows enough—which isn't all that much—to get into the film-making business."
2. **(2) lively adventure books** The reviewer clearly liked the movie, which can certainly be described as lively. Since the movie involves criminals and various shady characters, one can assume there is some aspect of adventure.

PAGE 49

3. **(3) Beloved is Sethe's guest. (*Comprehension: Detail*)** This option is supported by the statement in the passage, "the company of this sweet, if peculiar, guest pleased her."
4. **(4) read the book several times (*Application*)** Beloved is infatuated with Sethe and wants to be in Sethe's company as much as possible. If Beloved read an excellent book, she would be likely to stay with the book as much as possible—by rereading it several times.
5. **(1) the extent of Beloved's feelings for Sethe (*Analysis: Character*)** The description of how attentive Beloved is to Sethe's every move gives some idea about Beloved's character.
6. **(2) compassionate, with a painful history (*Synthesis: Additional Information*)** Sethe exhibits a pleasant and compassionate reaction to Beloved's sweet devotion. But with additional information about Sethe's past, a more complex view of Sethe emerges—one with a painful history.

READING MINI-TEST

PAGE 51

1. **(4) Keys is a multi-talented new artist who puts on a great show. (*Comprehension: Main Idea*)** This option summarizes the reviewer's main point and supporting examples.
2. **(5) sometimes find great artists through sheer luck (*Comprehension: Implication*)** This conclusion is based on the reviewer's statement, "One can only imagine the shiver that ran down hit-maker Clive Davis' spine when he came across Keys. . ."

This implies that it was a lucky break that Davis found Keys.

3. **(4) a large concert hall** *(Analysis: Setting)* Based on the description of the set, the size of the band, and the dance numbers, this concert was most likely performed in a large concert hall.

4. **(2) impressed if the person were talented** *(Application)* This question essentially asks whether the reviewer would enjoy an entire concert with a solo singer/song-writer/performer—without the band and dancing that was also part of Keys' concert. The reviewer noted that the solo part of Keys' performance was "an exclamation point" to her concert.

5. **(2) passionate** *(Synthesis: Tone)* The reviewer revealed her passionate appreciation of Key's work by choosing such words as "stunning," "oozing charisma," "lush songs," "took home an armload of Grammys," "band's formidable musicianship," "biggest crowd-pleasers," and "the evening's arguable highlight."

6. **(3) at ease with it** *(Comprehension: Inference)* The reviewer states that "Keys wears all that commercial and critical success as easily as her signature sequined fedoras." This implies that Keys is at ease with her success.

PAGE 53

7. **(5) an outside narrator** *(Synthesis: Point of View)* The use of the characters' names and the third-person pronouns *he* and *him* indicate that an outside narrator is telling the story, not one of the characters.

8. **(4) He doesn't want Lamin to realize that he doesn't know the answer.** *(Analysis: Character)* Kunta enjoys answering Lamin's questions. It is only when Lamin asks him something that he doesn't know that he changes the subject, becomes quiet, or acts as though he is deep in thought.

9. **(4) They both ask a lot of questions.** *(Analysis: Comparison and Contrast)* Kunta asked a lot of questions of Omoro. Lamin is asking a lot of questions of Kunta, so many that he gets tired of answering.

10. **(3) stop talking to him** *(Application)* The last paragraph states that Mandinka home training taught that one never talked to someone who did not want to talk.

11. **(4) He wants to be like Kunta.** *(Analysis: Inference)* We see that Lamin is constantly asking Kunta questions. This indicates that he wants to know everything Kunta knows and therefore admires and probably wants to be like Kunta.

UNIT 2: SOCIAL STUDIES

LESSON 14

PAGE 57

Important Information
TOPIC: Soybean use and production
Made into food, fertilizer, and oil; high protein content Grown in China for over 4,000 years **First brought to U.S. in 1880** **Now grown around the world** **Over 50% grown in U.S.**

1. Soybeans have many uses including food, fertilizer, and oil. They are now being grown around the world.

2. The United States is the largest producer of soybeans in the world.

3. **(3) natural-born citizen, 35 years of age, 14 years of American residency** This answer restates the information given in the passage.

LESSON 15

PAGE 59

Stated Information	What I Already Know	Implication
As time passes, most stamps are used and thrown away or are damaged or lost.	Discard, damage, and loss decrease supply.	**The supply of very old stamps is low.**
One of the oldest postage stamps is a stamp issued in British Guiana in 1856. It is worth over $900,000.	Old items are often rare and valuable.	**The British Guiana stamp is very rare.**

1. Old stamps are not very common because most have been used and discarded, damaged, or lost over time.
2. The stamp has a high value because it is one of the oldest that exists, and thus is very rare.
3. **(4) extremely large and heavy** The information that it took large teams of men to move each stone, and that they dragged the stones implies that the stones were large and heavy.

LESSON 16

PAGE 61

1. a woman is demonstrating for the right to vote.
2. serious; determined
3. that women did not have equal rights with men, including the right to vote
4. **(2) It was taken in a city with a large number of immigrants.** The numerous signs for citizenship services indicate that there were probably many immigrants in the city.

SOCIAL STUDIES SKILLS PRACTICE 1

PAGE 62

1. **(2) In 1908, young children worked in factories.** *(U.S. History: Implication)* By combining the date of the photo with the content of the photo, a reasonable inference can be made that children worked in factories in 1908.
2. **(1) Child Labor in 1908** *(U.S. History: Restate/Summarize)* This photo shows young children as part of the workforce.
3. **(2) The Silk Road was an ancient trade route that connected China and the West.** *(World History: Restate/Summarize)* This information is stated in the passage.
4. **(5) travelers preferred using sea routes** *(World History: Implication)* The passage states that a sea passage was opened in the 15th century and that use of the Silk Road declined after its opening. This information implies that travelers preferred using sea routes.

PAGE 63

5. **(5) The Resettlement Administration offered farmers hope.** *(U.S. History: Implication)* The artist is implying that the work of the Administration would end the farmer's suffering.
6. **(3) a brief history of Liberia** *(World History: Restate/Summarize)* The passage gives an overview of the history of Liberia.
7. **(2) He supported government regulation.** *(U.S. History: Implication)* The fact that Roosevelt intervened in monopolies, labor disputes, and industries implies that he favored government regulation.

LESSON 17

PAGE 65

```
┌─────────────────────────────────────┐
│     First step to determine CPI       │
│  The Bureau of Labor Statistics chooses │
│  a "market basket" of typical goods    │
│  and services.                         │
└─────────────────────────────────────┘
                   │
                   ▼
┌─────────────────────────────────────┐
│              Next step                 │
│  A reference year is established and the │
│  cost of the "market basket" is        │
│  determined for that year.             │
└─────────────────────────────────────┘
                   │
                   ▼
┌─────────────────────────────────────┐
│              Next step                 │
│  The cost of the "market basket" is    │
│  determined for a later year.          │
└─────────────────────────────────────┘
                   │
                   ▼
┌─────────────────────────────────────┐
│              Final step                │
│  The costs for both years are compared │
│  to show the percentage change in the  │
│  cost of the "market basket".          │
└─────────────────────────────────────┘
```

1. **(3) appear at a hearing** The passage states that this is the next step after filling out the application.

LESSON 18

PAGE 67

Cause ⟶	Effect
The Soviet Union wanted to stop East Germans escaping to West Berlin.	The Soviet Union built a barrier between East Germany and West Berlin.
East Germany lifted emigration restrictions in 1989.	**Germans celebrated by destroying the Berlin Wall.**

1. to prevent the mass departure of East Germans into West Berlin
2. Germans celebrated by destroying the Berlin Wall.

3. **(1) a combination of income-tax cuts and spending increases** The passage states that deficits have often been a result of income-tax cuts (less money coming in) and spending increases.

LESSON 19

PAGE 69

Nile River	Both	Panama Canal
• Naturally occurring • Used for farming, fishing, raising animals • 50% can be navigated	• Waterways • Contribute to economy • Used by boats	• Man-made • Used for passage between oceans • 100% can be navigated

1. They are both waterways; they both contribute to their country's economy; at least some portion of both can be navigated by boats.
2. The Nile is naturally occurring, but the Panama Canal is man-made. The primary use of the Panama Canal is as a passage between oceans, but the primary uses of the Nile are for farming and fishing. Ships can travel the entire length of the Panama Canal, but only about half of the Nile.
3. **(4) They both dealt with property rights.** The passage says that the first section dealt with property, and the second section with the government's right to take private property for public use.

LESSON 20

PAGE 71

1. The map shows the routes and dates of two South Pole expeditions by Shackleton.
2. Shackleton came closer to the South Geographic Pole on his first expedition.
3. Shackleton began and ended his second expedition at South Georgia Island.
4. **(1) Copenhagen** Use the key to help identify capital cities. Copenhagen is the capital that is farthest south.

SOCIAL STUDIES SKILLS PRACTICE 2

PAGE 72

1. **(5) He traveled around China as the emperor's aide.** *(World History: Sequence of Events)* The passage states that Marco Polo traveled as the emperor's aide after befriending the emperor.
2. **(2) The Italians gained access to many Chinese innovations.** *(World History: Cause/Effect)* The passage explains how Marco Polo brought Chinese inventions to Italy.
3. **(3) Canada's are much lower.** *(Geography: Compare/Contrast)* The map shows that the temperatures in most of Canada are 14°F and lower, but the temperatures in most of Mexico range from 77°F to 41°F.
4. **(4) There is a much greater range of temperatures in the U.S.** *(Geography: Compare/Contrast)* The average daily temperature in Canada ranges from 41°F to less than 14°F, but the average daily temperature in the U.S. ranges from 68°F to below 14°F.

PAGE 73

5. **(5) European languages are spoken in much of South America.** *(Geography: Cause/Effect)* According to the map, European languages are spoken in a large portion of South America.
6. **(3) a map showing the European settlement of South America** *(Geography: Compare/Contrast)* It would show the link between the countries that settled South America and the languages being spoken.
7. **(4) The Bill of Rights was adopted.** *(Civics and Government: Sequence of Events)* After the Constitution was written, the Bill of Rights was drafted and then adopted.
8. **(3) Many Americans wanted the Constitution to provide protection for basic individual rights.** *(Civics and Government: Cause/Effect)* The passage states that many

people were displeased that the Constitution lacked protection for individual rights.

LESSON 21

PAGE 75

Important Details
• 1st national minimum wage laws: Fair Labor Standards Act, 1938
• Act set minimum wage at $0.25 an hour
• Act intended to stop wage cutting during Depression
• Congress has raised minimum wage 17 times
• 1950: $0.75 an hour; 1997: $5.15 an hour
• Opponents: minimum wage leads to rising inflation and fewer entry-level jobs

1. The passage mentions the opinions of some opponents of the laws. If there are opponents, then not everyone supports the laws.
2. Unemployment rates would need to be provided along with dates so that this data could be compared with the dates of minimum wage law changes. Reasons why employers cut jobs would also be helpful.
3. **(1) No, the total number of electricity users is needed.** While the passage does state that TVA dams provide hydroelectric power for over three million people, that number would need to be compared with the total number of electricity users in that region.

LESSON 22

PAGE 77

Event ——→	Prediction
• Illegal ivory trade increases	• More elephants are killed.
• Artificial ivory developed	• Less illegal ivory is used.

1. Poaching would increase, and large numbers of elephants would be killed.
2. More products would be made from artificial ivory, the use of illegal elephant ivory would decrease, and poaching would decrease.
3. **(4) keep the 1954 version of the pledge** If the majority of Americans (79%) supported keeping the words, the outcome of a national vote would likely be in favor of keeping the current version.

LESSON 23

PAGE 79

Idea from Given Information	Application to New Situation
The 1949 convention allowed for the establishment of a war crimes tribunal.	If former Yugoslavian leaders have committed war crimes, they could be tried by a war crimes tribunal.
Additional conventions have been added to establish international rules for actions during wartime.	If rules for distributing humanitarian aid during war were needed, a new convention could be added to the Geneva Conventions.

1. They could be accused and tried by a war crimes tribunal.
2. A new convention that established those rules could be added to the Geneva Conventions.
3. **(3) to protect the city from attack** The passage explains that the Great Wall was built to protect China from invasion. If this idea is applied to St. Augustine, it is likely that the wall was built for a similar purpose.

LESSON 24

PAGE 81

1. The graph compares the amount of gold held in reserve by Belgium and the United Kingdom during the 1990s.
2. 1990
3. The United Kingdom's gold reserves remained generally constant at approximately 25 million ounces for most of the 1990s. Its reserves rose to about 30 million ounces in 1998.
4. **(2) The cost will be greater than $16,000.** The graph shows a steady increase in tuition rates. If the graph were extended beyond 1999, it is likely that it would continue to rise each year. However, based on the graph, tuition is unlikely to quadruple in cost to $60,000.

SOCIAL STUDIES SKILLS PRACTICE 3

PAGE 82

1. **(1) a flag with a dark background, to signify space, and an American flag in the corner, to symbolize the history of the colonists** *(Civics and Government: Application)* The passage states that the design of a flag expresses the ideals, beliefs, and history of its bearer. Therefore, this flag would most likely reflect the ideals and history of the colonists.
2. **(5) to identify the soldiers' unit** *(Civics and Government: Application)* Flags are often used to identify nations and states. It is therefore reasonable to apply this concept to soldiers' patches.
3. **(2) No, more information about voting rates for people ages 18 to 20 and for people 21 and over is needed.** *(Civics and Government: Adequacy of Data)* The graph only shows the percentage of total voter participation; it does not show the voting rates for people in the two specific age groups.

4. **(4) data about the kind of equipment used in polar exploration with dates of invention** *(Geography: Adequacy of Data)* If invention dates of new technology used in polar exploration were compared to the dates of expeditions, a conclusion could be drawn about the effect of improved technology on the number of expeditions.

5. **(5) Antarctic expeditions will increase more than Arctic ones.** *(Geography: Predict Outcomes)* In the graph, Antarctic exploration has increased more than Arctic exploration since the 18th century. It is reasonable to predict that this trend will continue.

6. **(2) No, information about the number of people who use each card is needed.** *(Economics: Adequacy of Data)* If there were numbers for the use of each type of card, a comparison could lead to a conclusion about which card is preferred.

7. **(3) a student loan for college** *(Economics: Application)* Like a credit card account, a loan for college tuition is not secured by collateral, since an education is not a concrete object.

LESSON 25

PAGE 85

Facts	Opinions
• Capital site chosen in 1791 by George Washington	• George Washington showed political brilliance
• Site close to geographic center of original 13 colonies	• One of the most important and beautiful cities in the U.S.
• Planned city; planned by L'Enfant	
• Sites designated for government buildings, monuments, and memorials	

1. **(1) Ted Turner is one of America's most successful businesspeople.** This statement shows beliefs, not facts.

LESSON 26

PAGE 87

Subject	Values and Beliefs
Continental Congress and Great Seal designers	• Believed that America needed an official seal • Valued 13 as a symbolic number • Valued peace and might
Today's government	• Values seal because it's only used on important diplomatic documents

1. peace and might
2. The fact that the seal is only used for important documents shows that the government values the seal as an important symbol of the United States.
3. **(5) The U.S. government values a free market.** The fact that the government bans monopolies, which compromise a free market, shows that the government values a free market.

LESSON 27

PAGE 89

1. The topic of this cartoon is the federal government's economic and environmental policies.
2. The tree represents the environment, or damage to the environment or the nation's natural resources.
3. John Sherffius thinks that government policies that allow damage to the environment are enriching wealthy corporations and Americans.
4. **(3) Because of media coverage, Americans today can view wars as they happen, rather than as programs at a later

date. The cartoon shows Americans watching military action on television, as it happens. The dialogue contrasts the immediate viewing of events with the fact that, in the past, many events were not viewed by the public until they were presented as historical documentaries.

SOCIAL STUDIES SKILLS PRACTICE 4

PAGE 90

1. **(3) Less successful cultures only recently began using coins and paper currency.** *(Economics: Fact and Opinion)* It is an opinion that cultures late to use a money system are "less successful" because ideas will differ on what makes a culture "successful."

2. **(5) Both coins and paper currency have been used for 1,000 years or more.** *(Economics: Fact and Opinion)* This is a fact because it can be proven to be true.

3. **(1) Many ancient cultures valued an organized system of currency.** *(Economics: Values and Beliefs)* This is shown by statements in the passage.

4. **(4) civil rights** *(Civics and Government: Implication)* In this cartoon, the Constitution represents rights, such as trial by jury, being run over by military tribunals.

PAGE 91

5. **(5) the American nation, preparing for war** *(Civics and Government: Implication)* The eagle is often a symbol of the United States. The eagle is sharpening its claws as a symbol of preparing to fight back.

6. **(1) The American people are strong and determined.** *(Civics and Government: Fact and Opinion)* By showing the eagle with exaggerated muscles, sharpened claws, and a resolved look on its face, the artist conveys his opinion that the nation is strong and determined.

7. **(4) Town meetings in a large city would certainly be inefficient and chaotic.** *(Civics and Government: Fact and Opinion)* This statement is an opinion because it expresses a belief that is not necessarily true.

8. **(3) Town meetings allow each citizen to speak, debate, and vote on legislation.** *(Civics and Government: Adequacy of Data)* Allowing every citizen the right to directly participate in government is an example of direct democracy.

SOCIAL STUDIES MINI-TEST

PAGE 92

1. **(4) Franklin and Gettysburg** *(U.S. History: Compare/Contrast)* Franklin had the lowest Union casualties; Gettysburg, the highest. Union casualties were approximately equal in the other three battles.

2. **(2) Gettysburg, Antietam** *(U.S. History: Sequence)* The Confederate casualty ranking, from highest to lowest, was Gettysburg, Antietam, Shiloh, Franklin, and Fredericksburg.

3. **(5) Division of labor requires specialization among workers.** *(Economics: Fact/Opinion)* Only option 5 is a statement of fact and is supported by the third sentence.

4. **(1) automobile assembly line workers** *(Economics: Application)* On an automobile assembly line, each step in the process is performed by a worker who specializes in that task. There may be a small degree of specialization in the other options, but the workers do not participate in the step-by-step production of a product.

PAGE 93

5. **(3) pollution and careless fishing practices** *(Geography: Cause/Effect)* The passage mentions the harm caused by dumping waste, overfishing, and using dynamite.

6. **(4) Coral reefs and algae-eating fish have a mutually supportive relationship.** *(Geography: Adequacy of Data)* The reference to coral being smothered when fishers have caught too many algae-eating fish supports this statement.

7. **(3) Both show violent tendencies.** *(World History: Compare/Contrast)* The cat is holding a dead dove (which it can be assumed to have killed) in its mouth; the angry dog is trying to catch the cat. No details in the cartoon support the other options.

8. **(5) Strife between the Palestinians and the Israelis has gone on for some time.** *(World History: Implication)* The deep circular indentation in the ground indicates that a cycle of violence has been going on for some time.

PAGE 94

9. **(2) A census is valuable in many ways.** *(Civics and Government: Restate/ Summarize)* The passage discusses several uses of the census.

10. **(3) Syria, and Jordan have no oil.** *(Geography: Compare/ Contrast)* The symbol for oil does not appear in these two countries.

11. **(1) Several countries would face severe economic problems.** *(Geography: Predict Outcomes)* The loss of a market for oil would hit oil-producing countries hard.

PAGE 95

12. **(5) patriotism and equality** *(Civics and Government: Values and Beliefs)* The concepts are reflected in the key elements of a flag, an honor roll of multicultural names, and the words *Americans All!*

13. **(3) more Asian and Latino names** *(Civics and Government: Application)* Since the poster strongly implies the acceptance of all ethnic groups, an updated poster would probably attempt to do the same.

14. **(4) "For a long time I have known that white men would defeat us."** *(U.S.*

History: Restate/Summarize) Chief Joseph speaks of a long-held belief, and he compares white men to predatory beasts. Options 2 and 5 address only parts of the comment, and options 1 and 3 do not address it at all.

15. **(2) He gained the respect of many officials.** *(U.S. History: Cause/Effect)* The respect he gained because of his courage was not Chief Joseph's objective, but it is what he achieved.

UNIT 3: SCIENCE

LESSON 28

PAGE 99

OBSERVATIONS	QUESTION	TEST/RESEARCH	CONCLUSIONS
People say that heavy things fall faster than light things.	Do heavy things fall faster than light things?	Measure how long it takes heavy and light balls to fall to the ground from a tower	Weight does not affect how fast things fall. Falling objects of differ weights reach the ground in the same amount of time.

1. Do heavy things fall faster than light things?

2. Weight does not affect how fast things fall. Falling objects of different weights reach the ground in the same amount of time.

3. **(4) What effect do CFCs have on the atmosphere?** This is the question that scientists investigated first and that led to the prediction of an ozone hole.

LESSON 29

PAGE 101

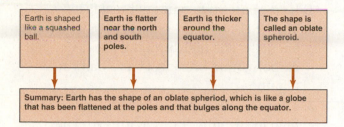

1. Earth has the shape of a squashed ball.
2. Earth is an oblate spheroid because it is flatter at the poles and it bulges along the equator.
3. **(3) Matter is anything that has mass and volume.** This answer best summarizes the information in the first paragraph.

LESSON 30

PAGE 103

1. The main topic of the table is different types of suspensions (solid, liquid, or gas).
2. whipped cream, marshmallows
3. Suspensions are mixtures of particles scattered throughout a substance.
4. **(5) 7** According to the table, many buildings crumble at this level.

SCIENCE SKILLS PRACTICE 1

PAGE 104

1. **(4) Can touch therapists feel energy fields?** *(Life Science: Scientific Method)* This is the question that Rosa's experiment tested.
2. **(2) TT therapists cannot detect energy fields.** *(Life Science: Restate)* Rosa's published paper stated that her experiments were evidence that TT practitioners cannot feel energy fields.
3. **(3) Asia** *(Earth and Space Science: Tables)* According to the table, Asia's highest point

is 8,846 feet, much higher than the highest points on the other continents.

4. **(4) The highest points on each continent vary in height by thousands of meters.** *(Earth and Space Science: Summarize)* This answer best summarizes the information in the table, which is about heights of the highest mountain on each continent.

PAGE 105

5. **(4) Each cup of cereal is one serving.** *(Life Science: Restate)* According to the table, the serving size is one cup.
6. **(3) Measure the number of cups of cereal in the box.** *(Life Science: Scientific Method)* Measuring the amount of cereal in the box is the best way to test the reported volume.
7. **(5) In dry cleaning, clothes are washed with a chemical instead of water.** *(Physical Science: Summarize)* The passage is about the benefits of dry cleaning clothes with tetrachloroethylene.
8. **(1) It gets rid of stains and is less harmful than some other dry cleaning chemicals.** *(Physical Science: Restate)* The passage says that this chemical gets out tough stains and is less toxic than others.

LESSON 31

PAGE 107

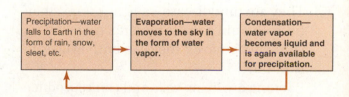

1. evaporation
2. condensation
3. **(3) Stretch muscles gently.** A gradual cooldown is the last step in the workout.

LESSON 32

PAGE 109

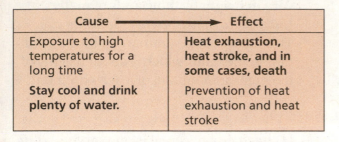

Cause	→	Effect
Exposure to high temperatures for a long time		Heat exhaustion, heat stroke, and in some cases, death
Stay cool and drink plenty of water.		Prevention of heat exhaustion and heat stroke

1. being exposed to high temperatures for a long time; doing physical activities in high temperatures
2. Stay cool by spending time in air-conditioned places and taking cool showers. Drink water. Limit activities to cooler times of the day.
3. (2) **The balloons have like charges.** Like charges repel.

LESSON 33

PAGE 111

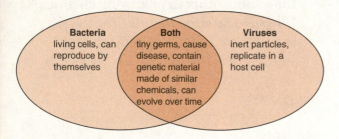

1. They are tiny, disease-causing germs; they both contain genetic material made of similar chemicals; they can both evolve over time.
2. Bacteria are living cells and can reproduce by themselves. Viruses are inert particles that require a host cell to replicate.
3. (4) **commonly recycled into new products** The passage mentions several items that can be made by recycling plastics coded 1 and 2.

LESSON 34

PAGE 113

1. It compares two types of breakfasts.
2. The USDA breakfast includes orange juice and jelly. The high-protein, low-carbohydrate breakfast has a half can-teloupe.
3. The main dish in the USDA breakfast is high in carbohydrates (oatmeal). The high-protein, low-carbohydrate main dish is high in protein (cheese and eggs).
4. (4) **The image is transferred to paper.** According to the diagram, after toner is attracted to the image area on the drum, the image is transferred to paper.

SCIENCE SKILLS PRACTICE 2

PAGE 114

1. (3) **how a submarine dives and rises** *(Physical Science: Diagrams)* The diagram's title is "How Ballast Tanks Work in a Submarine," and the diagram shows how ballast tanks open and close to help the submarine dive and surface.
2. (2) **pump air into the ballast tanks** *(Physical Science: Cause)* Air is pumped into the submarine's tanks to cause it to float to the surface.
3. (1) **many times greater than normal G-force** *(Physical Science: Contrast)* The passage says that normal G-force is 1-G and some new roller coasters have G-forces of 5-G and 6-G.
4. (2) **safer amusement park rides** *(Physical Science: Effect)* The passage mentions some possible physical injuries that can be caused by high G-forces. Limiting G-forces could prevent injuries, and therefore provide safer rides.

PAGE 115

5. **(4) waxing gibbous** *(Earth and Space Science: Sequence)* According to the diagram, waxing gibbous comes just before a full moon.

6. **(2) full moon** *(Earth and Space Science: Sequence)* A second full moon in one month is a blue moon. The cycle takes 29.5 days, so the first phase would have to be a full moon.

7. **(5) waning gibbous** *(Earth and Space Science: Sequence)* According to the diagram, waning gibbous comes just after a full moon. Since a blue moon is a full moon, it would be followed by a waning gibbous, too.

8. **(4) consist of carbon** *(Physical Science: Compare)* This is the only similarity mentioned in the passage.

9. **(2) press upward quickly but gently** *(Life Science: Sequence)* This is the last step according to the passage.

LESSON 35

PAGE 117

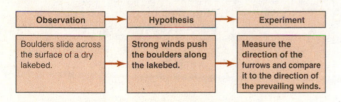

1. They hypothesized that strong winds push the boulders along the lakebed.

2. They carefully measured the direction of the furrows and compared it to the direction of the prevailing winds.

3. **(3) The *T/S Command* was in the vicinity just before the slick appeared.** According to the passage, officials hypothesized that the oil came from the *T/S Command* because they knew the ship was at the scene of the crime right before it happened.

LESSON 36

PAGE 119

1. Muscles that are used to support the body's weight against gravity fatigue slowly.

2. Since neck muscles keep the head upright, they are supporting the body's weight against gravity. According to the passage, such muscles fatigue slowly.

3. **(4) destruction of buildings and trees** With wind speeds of more than 300 miles per hour, tornadoes can be even more destructive than category 5 hurricanes.

LESSON 37

PAGE 121

1. the energy content of selected foods
2. 50 calories
3. nonfat yogurt
4. **(2) Smoking cigarettes increases the risk of getting lung cancer.** According to the graph, the more cigarettes a person smokes per day, the greater the risk of getting lung cancer.

SCIENCE SKILLS PRACTICE 3

PAGE 122

1. **(1) Battery life decreases as temperature decreases.** *(Physical Science: Summarize)* According to the graph, battery life is short at low temperatures and long at high temperatures.

2. **(4) Flashlights work longer in warm weather.** *(Physical Science: Application)*

ANSWERS AND EXPLANATIONS

Flashlights use batteries, which last longer at higher temperatures.

3. **(3) An earthquake near Washington or Oregon caused the Japanese tsunami.** *(Earth and Space Science: Hypothesis)* According to the information given, scientists proposed that the Japanese tsunami was caused by a large earthquake that occurred near Washington or Oregon.

4. **(5) They studied the growth rings of old, dead trees.** *(Earth and Space Science: Hypothesis)* According to the information given, scientists studied the growth rings of old, dead trees along the Washington coast.

PAGE 123

5. **(4) Cleaners with antibiotics are more effective at killing bacteria.** *(Life Science: Hypothesis)* The scientist tested two cleaners that contained antibiotics and two cleaners that did not.

6. **(2) Cleaners with antibiotics were most effective at killing bacteria.** *(Life Science: Restate)* The bars for cleaners A and B are higher than those for C and D, indicating a greater percent of bacteria killed.

7. **(2) a solar-powered calculator** *(Physical Science: Application)* A solar-powered calculator runs on electricity produced when light is absorbed by a panel on the calculator.

8. **(3) the development of a legless, fishlike tadpole into a frog** *(Life Science: Application)* A tadpole changes its form when it develops into a frog.

LESSON 38

PAGE 125

If	Then
1. The layers are arranged in order of their age. 2. The layer at the top is the youngest. 3. The Redwall limestone is below the Kaibab limestone.	The Redwall limestone is **older than the Kaibab limestone.**

1. The Redwall limestone is older than the Kaibab limestone.
2. The Redwall limestone formed between 280 million and 500 million years ago.
3. **(4) FM radio waves pass through the ionosphere.** According to the passage, FM radio waves have wavelengths between 0.1 and 10 meters, and waves that have wavelengths less than 10 meters pass through the ionosphere.

LESSON 39

PAGE 127

Conclusion	Phenolics are good materials for making cookware handles.
Supporting data	1. Phenolics retain shape at high temperatures. 2. Phenolics are poor heat conductors.

1. Phenolics are good materials for making cookware handles.
2. No. The passage tells about how the pans cook food, but not about how the metal stands up to heat and water.
3. **(1) The plains in the area are made of rock and gravel.** According to the passage, the finely ground rock and gravel were deposited by the glacier.

LESSON 40

PAGE 129

1. the percentage of people with diabetes who use different medicines
2. 22%
3. **a**
4. **(5) The atmosphere contains very little oxygen.** The graph shows that oxygen makes up less than 1% of Mars' atmosphere.

SCIENCE SKILLS PRACTICE 4

PAGE 130

1. **(3) Carbohydrates provide the most calories. *(Life Science: Restate)*** According to the graph, 46 percent of the calories come from carbohydrates, which is more than the percentages given for fats or proteins.
2. **(4) This diet does not meet nutrition experts' recommendation for a healthful diet. *(Life Science: Conclusions)*** Fats provide 42 percent of the calories in this diet, which is greater than the percentage that nutrition experts recommend for a healthful diet.
3. **(2) Helium is nonflammable. *(Physical Science: Adequacy of Data)*** Unlike helium, hydrogen is flammable, and airships that contained hydrogen have burned.
4. **(5) It is denser than hot air. *(Physical Science: Conclusions)*** According to the passage, hot air makes balloons rise. In addition, gases that are less dense than air rise. If carbon dioxide makes balloons sink, it must be denser than hot air.

PAGE 131

5. **(2) Coals from both mines contain oxygen. *(Earth and Space Science: Summarize)*** The graphs show that coal from mine A contains 7% oxygen and coal from mine B contains 15%.

6. **(1) Coal from mine A contains more carbon. *(Earth and Space Science: Adequacy of Data)*** The graphs show that coal from mine A contains 66% carbon, and coal from mine B contains 45% carbon. According to the passage, the more carbon a sample of coal contains, the more energy it produces.
7. **(4) It turns litmus paper red. *(Physical Science: Adequacy of Data)*** Substances that have a pH less than 7 are acids and turn litmus paper red. This is the only conclusion that can be verified by the facts given.
8. **(3) There are ancient beaches on slopes above the ocean. *(Earth and Space Science: Conclusions)*** Ancient beaches on slopes above the Pacific Ocean show that these slopes were once below sea level, so sea level must have been higher then.

SCIENCE MINI-TEST

PAGE 132

1. **(1) What causes pellagra? *(Life Science: Science as Inquiry: Analysis)*** Goldberger wanted to know the causes of pellagra so he could prevent and treat it.
2. **(3) Pellagra results from a poor diet. *(Life Science: History and Nature of Science: Comprehension)*** Goldberger's experiments all linked diet to pellagra.
3. **(5) a lack of vitamin B *(Life Science: Science in Social and Personal Perspectives: Analysis)*** After Goldberger died, it was shown that vitamin B cured pellagra.
4. **(2) last a week or longer. *(Earth and Space Science: Science in Social and Personal Perspectives: Analysis)*** According to the table, hurricanes last about one week, and cyclones last one week or longer as well.

PAGE 133

5. **(4) The air bag inflates with nitrogen gas. *(Physical Science: Science as Inquiry:***

Analysis) According to the diagram, this is the last step.

6. **(5) The air bag inflates.** *(Physical Science: Science as Inquiry: Analysis)* The nitrogen gas flowing into the bag causes it to inflate.

7. **(4) Common names are different in different languages.** *(Life Science: Unifying Concepts and Processes: Analysis)* Common names vary from place to place whereas scientific names are always the same.

8. **(5) Scientific names are made up of two Latin words, which tell the genus and the species of an organism.** *(Life Science: Unifying Concepts and Processes: Comprehension)* The second paragraph gives details about scientific names.

PAGE 134

9. **(3) The number of tornadoes rises from January through May.** *(Earth and Space Science: Unifying Concepts and Processes: Comprehension)* The lengths of the bars increase from January through May, which means that the number of tornadoes increases during these months. The other options disagree with the information in the graph.

10. **(2) Tornadoes are most likely to occur in May and June.** *(Earth and Space Science: Science in Social and Personal Perspectives: Analysis)* The graph shows that tornadoes occur most often in May and June.

11. **(4) Macaroni takes longer to cook in Denver.** *(Physical Science: Science and Technology: Application)* Macaroni cooks in boiling water. Because boiling water is less hot in Denver than at sea level, macaroni will take longer to cook in Denver.

12. **(2) It is very resistant to weathering.** *(Earth and Space Science: Science and Technology: Evaluation)* The fact that granite is very resistant to weathering means that it does not break down quickly when exposed to wind and rain. This fea-

ture is useful for monuments, which are intended to last a long time.

PAGE 135

13. **(1) There are more cedars after 250 years than after 25 years.** *(Life Science: Unifying Concepts and Processes: Comprehension)* Cedars make up 40 percent of the 250-year-old forest but only 4 percent of the 25-year-old forest.

14. **(4) The first trees to grow back after a fire are hardwoods.** *(Life Science: Science as Inquiry: Analysis)* According to the graphs, hardwoods make up 83 percent of the forest 25 years after a fire.

15. **(3) an automatic door activated by an electric eye** *(Physical Science: Science and Technology: Application)* An electric eye opens a door when a person or some object blocks the light that the electric eye senses.

16. **(5) They examined six dead whales.** *(Life Science: Science in Social and Personal Perspectives: Analysis)* According to the passage, the scientists hypothesized that the whales became stranded because their ears were injured. By examining the heads of some of the dead whales, the scientists were able to look for such injuries.

POSTTEST

UNIT 1: READING

PAGE 136

1. **(3) The birds were making an insane attack.** *(Fiction: Comprehension)* Almost all of the passage deals with the birds attacking Nat and his trying to get away. The birds' behavior can be described as insane because they are attacking Nat for no apparent reason and dying in the process.

2. **(1) There were a lot of birds.** *(Fiction: Comprehension)* The birds were attacking Nat, so it makes sense that he was swing-

ing at them with the hoe. The hoe would likely scare off one or two birds, but not a swarm.

3. **(5) to show that the attacks will worsen** *(Fiction: Synthesis)* The word "yet" shows that the birds will learn how to do these things in the future, and this knowledge is sure to make the attacks worse and more deadly. The attack Nat is experiencing is already very serious.

4. **(3) He would wrap his wound and get help.** *(Fiction: Application)* Nat is protecting his most vulnerable areas (eyes and head) and trying to get somewhere safe. He is not wild, frantic, confused, or overconfident. If he cut himself, he would probably exhibit the same behavior—protecting the wound and getting help.

PAGE 137

5. **(5) Cannon wants to provide the best service to the university community.** *(Nonfiction: Comprehension)* This is clearly stated in the passage and supports the idea that Cannon emphasizes customer service.

6. **(4) friendly and casual** *(Nonfiction: Analysis)* The first paragraph welcomes the employees. The second paragraph contains phrases such as "part of our team" and "you will meet new friends."

7. **(3) Students would work there.** *(Nonfiction: Application)* Based on their history of hiring student workers, you could expect that they would also hire students to work in the art museum.

8. **(2) Students get excellent work experience.** *(Nonfiction: Analysis)* The employer, Cannon University Dining Services, expresses its expectation that students behave professionally, take responsibility, and anticipate needs on the job. You could therefore draw the conclusion that students will get good work experience there.

9. **(5) He has camped before.** *(Fiction: Analysis)* Nick knows how to make a comfortable campsite, and he does it in an organized, calm manner.

10. **(2) before he put up his tent** *(Fiction: Analysis)* The text clearly shows that he laid down his blankets to make his bed before he tied the rope and cut the pegs to put up the tent.

11. **(2) orderly and organized** *(Fiction: Analysis)* He's hungry but he still carefully takes steps to make a comfortable sleeping place for the night. This shows that he is organized and orderly, not impulsive.

12. **(3) He carefully made his bed, smoothing out any lumps.** (*Fiction: Synthesis*) The author chooses words that show a man who cares about sleeping on a smooth surface and takes the time to make sure the bed is just right.

PAGE 139

13. **(3) This novel is so engaging that you may need to read it twice.** (*Nonfiction: Comprehension*) The review suggests that you might race through the novel because the characters are compelling and the plot is intriguing. It then says, "your curiosity satisfied, . . . you can settle down for that second, slow reading."

14. **(4) They are both interested in Georgie.** *(Nonfiction: Synthesis)* The reviewer refers to a love triangle and notes that Georgie is living with Jim but is drawn to Luther.

15. **(4) romantic and powerful** *(Nonfiction: Application)* The reviewer enjoys the elements in this story: "love and music and the allure of each," "compelling characters," and "intriguing plot." We can guess that the reviewer would enjoy these same elements in artwork.

16. **(2) enthusiastic** (*Nonfiction: Synthesis*) The reviewer thinks that the novel is good enough to read twice.

UNIT 2: SOCIAL STUDIES

PAGE 140

17. **(2) In the early feudal period, samurai men and their wives had some equality.** *(World History: Comprehension)* The summary statement echoes line 2, the passage's topic sentence. Options 1, 3, and 5 merely address some of the details in the passage. The passage does not support option 4.

18. **(1) better-defended samurai property** *(World History: Analysis)* The passage says that these women could "protect their households from enemy attack."

19. **(4) flooding** *(Geography: Analysis)* The stilts lift the house above the level of minor floods. The stilts would offer no protection against options 1, 2, or 3 and probably option 5.

20. **(2) including tornado-safe rooms in new homes** *(Geography: Application)* Like stilts, tornado-safe rooms are a form of protection against severe weather.

PAGE 141

21. **(5) The United States is better than other countries.** *(U.S. History: Evaluation)* The passage relates the "Space Race" to the desire to prove American superiority.

22. **(3) the start of the Cold War** *(U.S. History: Analysis)* The chronological sequence of events is as follows: the start of the Cold War, the launch of *Sputnik I,* the flight of the first astronaut, the first unmanned lunar mission, and the American landing on the moon.

23. **(4) During this period, unemployment varied more in Canada than in the United States.** *(Economics: Comprehension)* After a peak in 1975, the U.S. unemployment rate gradually dropped; at the same time, Canada's rate went up and down more than once.

24. **(2) 1975** *(Economics: Analysis)* In 1975, the unemployment rate was higher in the U.S. than in Canada. At each of the other dates the rate was higher in Canada.

PAGE 142

25. **(1) People have died in accidents caused by drivers using cell phones.** *(Civics and Government: Analysis)* The cartoonist equates the combination of cars and cell phones with death. Each of the other options expresses an opinion.

26. **(3) Using a cell phone while driving is as dangerous as a loaded gun.** *(Civics and Govenment: Evaluation)* Guns plus bullets and *cars plus cell phones*, both resulting in death, indicates that the cartoonist believes they are both equally dangerous.

27. **(2) An uneducated child will probably achieve little as an adult.** *(U.S. History: Comprehension)* This idea is expressed by the first sentence.

28. **(5) multicultural education in schools** *(U.S. History: Application)* The point of the second paragraph is that the concept of "separate but equal" is not acceptable. Only option 5 supports the concept of cultural diversity.

PAGE 143

29. **(4) a largely Muslim population** *(World History: Analysis)* The map shows the religious makeup of the population, so options 1 and 2 can be eliminated. West and East Pakistan are shown as almost exclusively Muslim.

30. **(3) Hindus fleeing to India** *(World History: Analysis)* The most logical prediction would be to have people who found themselves in the religious minority feeling threatened and therefore moving to a place where their faith was better represented. Indeed, at the time of partition, many Hindus migrated into India and many Indian Muslims migrated into Pakistan.

31. **(1) It is foolish to lease a car instead of buying one.** *(Economics: Analysis)* Option 1 expresses a point of view; arguments could made both for and against it. Option 2 is not discussed. Options 3, 4, and 5 are factual statements.

32. **(2) Buying a car is often more economical than leasing one.** *(Economics: Evaluation)* The passage states that there is an economic benefit to buying a car if you plan to drive it more than five years or 15,000 miles a year.

UNIT 3: SCIENCE

PAGE 144

33. **(5) The largest component of soil A is sand.** *(Earth and Space Science: Science as Inquiry: Evaluation)* Soil A consists of 60 percent sand. Soils that contain a lot of sand have many pore spaces, so they are well aerated.

34. **(1) making bricks, tiles, and pottery** *(Earth and Space Science: Science and Technology: Application)* Soil B consists of 65 percent clay. Soils that contain a lot of clay are very hard when they are dry. Hardness is needed for bricks, tiles, and pottery.

35. **(3) Most estuaries are much smaller than they once were.** *(Life Science: Science in Social and Personal Perspectives: Evaluation)* Most estuaries are smaller because large areas have been drained and filled in to make new land for buildings and farms.

PAGE 145

36. **(4) It will form in the southeast.** *(Earth and Space Science: Science as Inquiry: Evaluation)* Each new volcano is formed as the crust moves northwest over the hot spot in the mantle. You can conclude that the next volcano will form southeast of what is now the youngest volcano in the chain.

37. **(3) Buntings navigate by using the stars.** *(Life Science: Science as Inquiry: Analysis)* The word "proposed" tells you that this idea was a hypothesis.

38. **(2) using three listeners in different places to find a bird that can be heard but not seen** *(Earth and Space Science: Science as Inquiry: Application)* Three listeners can find a bird by listening for the sounds produced by the bird in the same way that three seismic recording stations can locate an earthquake's epicenter by detecting waves produced by the earthquake.

39. **(3) Driving slowly is more economical.** *(Physical Science: Science as Inquiry: Analysis)* According to the graph, the car gets more miles per gallon of fuel the more slowly it is driven. This means it is more economical to drive slowly.

PAGE 146

40. **(4) –26°F** *(Earth and Space Science: Science in Social and Personal Perspectives: Analysis)* If you locate 0° and 30 mph on the table and follow across and down, the row and column intersect at –26°F.

41. **(3) wind and cold** *(Earth and Space Science: Science as Inquiry: Analysis)* According to the passage, wind chill is the rate of heat lost from a person's skin by wind and cold.

42. **(4) They were both discovered when they were accidentally tasted.** *(Physical Science: History and Nature of Science: Analysis)* According to the passage, both sweeteners were discovered accidentally.

43. **(3) tasting a substance accidentally spilled on fingers** *(Physical Science: History and Nature of Science: Comprehension)* Observations include seeing, smelling, tasting, hearing, or touching something. Aspartame was tasted on the finger of a researcher working on anti-ulcer drugs.

PAGE 147

44. **(4) The coils in the air conditioner absorb the heat.** *(Physical Science: Science and Technology: Comprehension)* The diagram shows the liquid in the air conditioner's coils evaporates, absorbing heat in the room.

45. **(1) Heat inside the house is moved outside of the house.** *(Physical Science: Science and Technology: Comprehension)* Heat is absorbed by evaporating liquid and then given off outside when the gas condenses.

46. **(5) reduces inflammation** *(Life Science: Science in Social and Personal Perspectives: Analysis)* Ibuprofen reduces inflammation, but acetaminophen does not.

47. **(1) help to preserve the natural world** *(Physical Science: Unifying Concepts and Processes: Comprehension)* The last sentence says that batteries do not end up in landfills, and so they help to preserve the natural world—which is another way of saying that they are better for the environment.

Acknowledgments

p. 4 Excerpt from *The Great Santini* by Pat Conroy. Copyright © 1976 by Pat Conroy. Reprinted by permission of Houghton Mifflin Company. All rights reserved.

p. 20 From *The Grapes of Wrath* by John Steinbeck, copyright 1939, renewed © 1967 by John Steinbeck. Used by permission of Viking Penguin, a division of Penguin Putnam, Inc.

p. 28 Excerpt from "Love Story Lifts 'Episode II'" by Margaret A. McGurk from the Cincinnati Enquirer, May 17, 2002. Reprinted by permission of Cincinnati Enquirer.

p. 29 Excerpt from *Wise Blood* by Flannery O'Connor. Copyright © 1962 by Flannery O'Connor. Copyright renewed © 1990 by Regina O'Connor. Reprinted by permission of Farrar, Straus and Giroux, LLC.

p. 34 Excerpt from *The Two Towers* by J.R.R. Tolkien. Copyright © 1954, 1965, 1966 by J.R.R. Tolkien. Copyright © renewed 1982 by Christopher R. Tolkien, Michael H.R. Tolkien, John F.R. Tolkien and Priscilla M.A.R. Tolkien. 1965/1966 editions copyright © renewed 1993, 1994 by Christopher R. Tolkien, John F.R. Tolkien and Priscilla M.A.R. Tolkien. Reprinted by permission of Houghton Mifflin Company. All rights reserved.

p. 35 Excerpt from "How Should One Read A Book?" in *The Second Common Reader* by Virginia Woolf, copyright 1932 by Harcourt, Inc. and renewed 1960 by Leonard Woolf, reprinted by permission of the publisher.

p. 42 From *Portnoy's Complaint* by Philip Roth, copyright © 1969, 1997 by Philip Roth. Used by permission of Random House, Inc.

p. 43 Excerpt from "Marvel-ous," a review of the Spider Man" movie by Jonathan Foreman from the New York Post, May 3rd, 2002. © 2002 NYP Holdings Inc., D/B/A New York Post. Reprinted by permission

p. 48 Excerpt from review of "Get Shorty" by Ralph Novak, *People Weekly,* 10/30/95. Copyright © 1995 Time Inc. Reprinted by permission.

p. 49 From *Beloved* by Toni Morrison. Reprint by permission of International Creative Management Inc. Copyright © 1987 by Toni Morrison.

p. 50 Excerpt from "Keys Blends Hits with Covers; Jams," by Gemma Tarlach, *Milwaukee Journal Sentinel,* July 3, 2002. Copyright © 2003 Journal Sentinel Inc., reproduced with permission.

p. 52 From *Roots* by Alex Haley, copyright © 1976 by Alex Haley. Used by permission of Doubleday, a division of Random House, Inc.

p. 136 From Daphne du Maurier's *Classics of the Macabre.* Copyright © Daphne du Maurier. Reprinted with permission of Curtis Brown Ltd., London, on behalf of the Chichester Partnership.

p. 138 From "Big Two-Hearted River: Part I." Reprinted with permission of Scribner, an imprint of Simon & Schuster Adult Publishing Group, from *The Short Stories by Ernest Hemingway.* Copyright © 1925 by Charles Scribner's Sons. Copyright © renewed 1953 by Ernest Hemingway.

p. 139 "Aussie novelist makes beautiful 'Music'" by Jean Patteson from *St. Paul Pioneer Press,* August 18, 2002. Reprinted by permission.